When the dust settled and the hot, red sun rose the next morning, Lincoln went to the Bull Run battlefield to survey the damage.

Nearly 800 corpses were scattered across the grassy field. Hundreds more soldiers, all of them about the age of Lincoln's oldest son, lay wounded and crying out for help. Lincoln put his head in his hands. This would be neither a quick nor an easy war.

"If Hell is not any more than this," Lincoln said through gritted teeth, "then Hell holds no terror for me."

A Background Note about *ABRAHAM LINCOLN: A Giant Among Presidents*

Abraham Lincoln was a great man and a great president. Many people think he was the greatest president the United States has ever had. Although he was born to very humble beginnings, Lincoln believed in himself and knew that, one day, he would make his mark in the wide world. Of all the things Lincoln loved and was interested in, he loved people and his country, perhaps, more than anything else. He believed there was nothing more important than treating people, all people, fairly and doing whatever we had to do to keep our country strong and unified. As a result, Lincoln would leave his mark by both preserving the United States as we know it and freeing millions of slaves.

Today, our country's love and remembrance of our sixteenth president can be seen all around us. Lincoln's face, sixty feet high, is carved into Mount Rushmore. Both the penny and the five-dollar-bill feature Lincoln. There are thirty-eight towns and six mountains named "Lincoln." And in Washington D.C., the towering Lincoln Memorial is our greatest tribute to the man known as "Honest Abe." Behind the twenty-foot of Lincoln are these words etched in white granite:

In This Temple
As In The Hearts Of The People
For Whom He Saved The Union
The Memory Of Abraham Lincoln
Is Enshrined Forever

Abraham LINCOLN

A Giant Among Presidents

TANYA SAVORY

 THE TOWNSEND LIBRARY

ABRAHAM LINCOLN
A Giant Among Presidents

TP THE TOWNSEND LIBRARY

For more titles in the Townsend Library,
visit our website: **www.townsendpress.com**

Printed in the United States of America

0 9 8 7 6 5 4 3 2 1

Townsend Press, Inc.
439 Kelley Drive
West Berlin, NJ 08091
permissions@townsendpress.com

ISBN-13: 978-1-59194-180-4
ISBN-10: 1-59194-180-6

Library of Congress Control Number:
2008943205

Contents

Prologue

It is 1809. The United States consists of only sixteen states, but there are new, wild areas to the west. Every day, more and more people take their chances and load up wagons to travel along dirt trails for weeks or even months in search of a better life. One of the greatest dangers these new settlers face is angry American Indians, whose lands continue to be brutally taken from them. Many Indians have now learned how to use guns, and they use them to protect their homes. Many others, believing that a person's soul is in their hair, still collect scalps. As a form of revenge, it becomes popular to kill and scalp Indians; and people begin to collect, buy, and trade Indian scalps as a hobby.

It is 1809. In New York City, pigs roam the streets, eating the mountains of garbage that are piled everywhere. Trash collection and indoor bathrooms are still many years away. Even so, the population of New York City doubles every ten years as thousands of immigrants arrive on ships. Like the settlers heading west, the immigrants are also looking for a better life. They have heard that this new country, the United States, offers more freedom and more opportunity. They have heard that part of the Declaration of Independence states, "All men are created equal." Wishing to escape countries where people are not treated equally, they continue to pour into America.

It is 1809. Doctors rarely understand why people get sick or how to cure sickness. The most common treatment for anything from a cold to cancer is "bleeding," since doctors believe that cutting a person and allowing blood to drain out will get rid of disease. Often, leeches are used to suck blood out of patients. Only ten years earlier, George Washington died of a simple sore throat after doctors bled him heavily four times, made him gargle with vinegar and butter, and placed a paste made of crushed beetles on his throat. Meanwhile, nearly a third of pregnant women die during or just after giving birth. It will be decades before doctors realize that washing their hands before delivering babies will save thousands of lives.

It is 1809. Later in the century, many things will be invented, including raincoats, balloons, bicycles, sewing machines, zippers, potato chips, toilet paper, and shoes that are actually made differently for right and left feet. Perhaps the best invention of all, in about twenty years, will be the match. But for now, people must strike flintstones together and hope for a spark that will start a fire. Most people simply keep a fire going day and night so that they will not have to build a new one. Since there is no such thing as electricity, a fire is absolutely necessary for everything from heat to light to cooking. And out in the areas of the country known as the "frontier," fires are often left burning outside all night long to ward off wild animals such as coyotes, wildcats, and panthers.

It was into this new and often difficult world that Abraham Lincoln was born on February 12, 1809. Sleet and cold rain fell on the roof of Nancy and Thomas Lincoln's one-room log cabin in the frontier land of Hodgenville, Kentucky. Two-year-old Sarah Lincoln sat near the fireplace as her father and her Aunt Betsy helped deliver her new baby brother. Childbirth was dangerous. Everyone in the room, except for little Sarah, knew that Nancy Lincoln or the baby might die. If something went terribly wrong, both might die. Few words were spoken, and Thomas Lincoln practically held his breath until Abraham's first cries were heard.

Gently, Abraham was placed on a bed made of piled cornhusks. The only blankets in the cabin were heavy bearskins.

"Baby girl?" Sarah asked carefully as her aunt covered Abraham up.

"No, dear," Aunt Betsy whispered. "It's a boy. It's your brother, Abraham."

"A boy!" Thomas Lincoln said happily. Thomas was a carpenter who built cabins. He also worked as a farmer, growing and raising everything the family ate. He had hoped for a son, someone to help him with all the hard work that never seemed to end in a life on the frontier.

Suddenly, accompanied by a burst of icy wind and sleet, Sarah's nine-year-old cousin, Dennis, opened the door and rushed in to see the new addition to the family. But when he looked at the long, thin baby, Dennis shook his head with a frown.

"Don't look like he'll ever be much," Dennis muttered. "Ain't much more than a string bean."

"Well, you wait and see," Thomas said, gazing down at Abraham. "Reckon he'll be a great cabin builder one day."

Little did Thomas and Nancy Lincoln know, on the stormy February morning in 1809, that one day their son would be much, much more than that.

Chapter 1

Six-year-old Abe Lincoln was in the field behind the family's cabin, helping his father plant squash and pumpkin seeds. Dark clouds hung low in the distance, and every few minutes Abe could hear a rumble of thunder echo through the Kentucky hills. When the lightning flashed, Abe would stop planting seeds and stare up at the sky. Sometimes he would become so fascinated by the oncoming storm that the sack of seeds would fall from his hands.

Abe's father, Thomas, looked at his son and shook his head. Laziness irritated him, and he wouldn't stand for it in his own son. "Abe! Pay attention. Stop playing around. We have to get these in the ground before the rain comes."

Abe jumped back to work, but as soon as the next boom of thunder reached him, he gazed at the sky again.

"What makes the thunder, Pa? Is the lightning making it?"

Thomas kept planting seeds. Growing up, he'd never gone to even a week of school. He couldn't read or write or sign his own name. And he certainly didn't know what caused thunder. More and more, Abe was asking questions that Thomas couldn't answer. *Foolish questions*, he thought. *That boy can waste half a day just thinking up new questions about things that don't matter.* Thomas looked at his own scarred and weathered hands as he planted. It took an incredible amount of work to live on the frontier. Daydreaming and laziness could ruin a man.

"I reckon that thunder is God's way of telling you to stop wasting time and get back to work!" Abe's father finally said angrily, his voice rising above the wind that was now blowing some of the seeds across the dry soil.

Abe worked in silence as the storm approached. When big drops of rain began to plop against his back, he looked at his father. Thomas just nodded at the last section of the field to indicate that they needed to finish the job, rain or not. As the rain began to fall harder, Abe worked faster. Soon, he was soaked to the skin, but he and his father moved side by side on the last row. Finally, all the seeds were planted.

Thomas reached over, patted his son's back, and pointed toward the cabin. Both ran quickly to the front door—a door that was only a bearskin hanging on four hooks. But as Thomas ducked into the dry cabin, Abe turned to see a tremendous flash of lightning followed almost immediately by a huge crash of thunder. Still curious, he stood there staring up at the sky as the downpour covered him, wondering why the thunder now came so quickly after the lightning. He might have stood there another hour if a big scarred hand hadn't reached out through the bearskin door and dragged him into the cabin.

"But I want to hear it again. I think I forgot some of it."

As Abe and his father sat drying themselves in front of the big fireplace, Abe begged his father to tell a story. Typically, Abe liked the stories best that had something to do with him. Abe's older sister, Sarah, and his mother also sat near the fire, trying to get enough light to mend clothes. The only window in the cabin was a small square covered with a yellowish waxy paper, and because of the storm outside, it was quite dark inside the one-room cabin except for the area right in front of the fire.

"Abe, I think you know that story by heart," Thomas said with a small smile. Despite his gruffness, Thomas loved to tell stories. He was known as one of the best storytellers in the small town of Knob Creek, Kentucky, where the Lincolns lived.

"All right, then," Thomas said with a wink to his wife. "Let me tell you a story about my father, your Grandfather Lincoln."

Abe's father began by describing the village in Green River, Kentucky, where he and his parents and three older brothers had lived many years ago. The Lincolns had been friends with Daniel Boone, and Thomas's father had heard many of Boone's stories about the fertile land in Kentucky. The family moved to Kentucky from Virginia and before long owned more than 5,000 acres.

"We were mighty well off . . . for a little while," Thomas said with sadness.

One morning, Thomas's father and three brothers were working out in the cornfield while eight-year-old Thomas tended to chickens nearby. Suddenly, a loud shot rang out, and Thomas heard his brothers yell. Thomas ran toward the field and saw his father on the ground, not moving at all. As his three brothers ran to the house for help, Thomas knelt by his father's side. He could see the blood pouring out of a bullet wound. Hearing footsteps, Thomas turned to see an Indian running toward him with a rifle in his hands. The Indian had streaks of paint down his face and a bright silver medallion hanging from a cord around his neck. Thomas froze in fear.

Just as the Indian came up beside Thomas and reached down to pick him up, another shot rang out. A bullet had pierced the medallion and gone into the Indian's heart. Thomas's oldest brother, who could shoot a squirrel from fifty yards away, had saved his baby brother's life. But their father lay dead in the cornfield.

"After that, things were never the same," Thomas said. "Within a few years, we all drifted in different directions. I was on my own at twelve years old, only six years older than you, Abe."

Abe just nodded, waiting for the best part.

"Your grandfather was a great man, Abe. That's why we named you after him—Abraham. Maybe someday you'll have a farm as big as his was."

Young Abraham rarely got the chance to go to school. As an adult, Lincoln looked back on his childhood and said, "I went to school by littles." By this, he meant that he went to school only now and then, a week here and a week there, but nothing that could be called a real education. Aside from the difficulty of the only school in Knob Creek being at the end of a three-mile walk through rough woods, Abe's father believed that education was a waste of time and made a boy soft and lazy.

"But he *wants* to learn," Nancy, Abe's mother, would gently argue. "It can't hurt to let him go to school for a while."

Thomas shook his head. "He can learn to read and write, but he don't need any more than that. Just so he can understand deeds to land and written agreements and such."

And so Abe walked along the creek to the schoolhouse whenever his father had no work for him to do, which was not very often. The school he attended consisted of one big room with dirt floors, rough wooden benches, and very few books or materials. In fact, there was rarely even a teacher. The students ranged in age from 6 to 18; those who knew more taught those who knew less. Now and then, an adult would show up and teach a lesson or two in between farming chores.

This kind of school was known as a "blab school" because everything was spoken or "blabbed" instead of written. There were no pencils, no paper, and no chalkboards. So when a child learned anything—from ABC's to multiplication—it was done by speaking and memorizing what was spoken. A blab school, with a few dozen students all talking at the same time, often sounded from a distance like a noisy beehive. Immediately, Abe was deeply drawn to learning. Even when he was only seven or eight years old, his mind was full of a million questions.

However, Abe had attended the school in Knob Creek only a handful of times before big changes in his life took place.

"I don't understand it, but they say this land isn't mine." One afternoon in 1817, Thomas Lincoln was holding up a piece of paper he couldn't read. Nancy looked at it and shook her head. She couldn't read it either, but she understood. Thomas was not the first man in this area to be told that the land he had paid for was not his. The laws of land ownership in Kentucky were vague and sketchy at best.

Thomas wadded up the paper and threw it angrily into the fire. "Don't matter," he said bitterly. "I hate this state anyway. I can't see staying in a state that still allows slavery, and that's for sure."

Nancy nodded. Both she and Thomas despised slavery, believing it to be cruel and morally wrong. Most of the Southern states were slave states. However, just north of

Kentucky, in Indiana, slavery was not allowed. Almost immediately, Thomas rode off alone toward Indiana to look for land. He could travel quickly on horseback, and in only a few days he had returned with news.

"I've found a place! Not more than a hundred miles up in Indiana in a little area called Pigeon Creek." Thomas was already packing as he spoke. Nancy, a quiet and often sad woman, only nodded again. When Thomas set his mind on something, she had no say in the matter. *One hundred miles, though!* she thought wearily. *That will take a week just to get there.*

But Nancy Lincoln was wrong. It took *two* weeks. Traveling through dense woods in a cart piled with all their belongings along a narrow, often unclear trail took an immense amount of time. Sarah and Nancy sat in the oxen-pulled cart while Abe and his father walked alongside it. At night, the family camped in the forest, wild animals snorting and howling in the woods around them. Abe was often in charge of making sure that the campfire did not go out. Fire would keep the bears and wildcats at a distance. More than once, eight-year-old Abe would awaken with a start, fearing that he had let the fire die, allowing hungry bears to surround the camp.

After two grueling weeks of travel, the Lincolns finally reached the new land that

Thomas had purchased. He had bought 160 acres, marked only by piles of brush and branches that he had left in the four corners of his land. It was no easy task locating a pile of sticks in the vast miles of open land, but Thomas eventually spotted one of his markers.

"This is it!" he shouted excitedly as he ran to the marker. He gestured toward the land in a wide sweep of his arm. "This is your new home."

Abe and Sarah looked around doubtfully. There were no other cabins in sight, no town, not even a road. It seemed very lonely.

"We'll build the cabin forty acres to the north of this marker, over near the woods," Thomas continued, walking quickly in that direction. "I found the perfect spot up on a hill."

The first thing Abe and his father did when the family reached the cabin site was to build what was known as a "half-face" camp. This was a simple shelter made from leaning two poles against a heavy tree branch and covering one side with bark and sticks. The other side of the shelter was completely open. Beds were made of leaves, and the floor was dirt. Small animals and any number of bugs wandered in and out of the shelter at all hours, but a fire built on the open side kept larger, dangerous animals at a distance.

As Abe and his father built the shelter, Sarah and Nancy began to unpack. The first item out of the wagon was a heavy water bucket. Suddenly, Nancy stood very still as though listening for something. Then her brow wrinkled with worry.

"Thomas! Where's the water? I don't hear a creek."

"I'll dig a well tomorrow. Folks say there's plenty of water in the land," Thomas called back. "The creek's just down the hill."

But "just down the hill" turned out to be more than a mile away. And the water that Thomas thought would be in the land could never be found, even after digging numerous holes. So, for the next ten years, one of Abe's many daily chores would be walking the long trail to Pigeon Creek to fill the heavy water bucket.

That winter of 1817 was terribly cold. Life in the half-face shelter was almost unbearable. Bitter winds and drifts of snow blew right in and on top of the family as they tried to sleep at night. Nonetheless, Abe and his father were up very early every morning, working on the family's cabin. Looking back on that year, Lincoln later wrote: "Though very young, I was large for my age, and had an axe put into my hands at once. And from that until within my twenty-third year, I was almost constantly handling that most useful instrument."

Spring finally came to the Pigeon Creek area, and along with it came Abe's aunt and uncle, Betsy and Tom Sparrow. Best of all, Abe's cousin, Dennis, was with them. Although Dennis was ten years older than Abe, the two boys became close friends, exploring the surrounding woods and sharing their fears and joys of growing up on the frontier. The Sparrows moved into the half-face shelter that spring as the Lincolns finally moved into their cabin. It was a spring and summer of more backbreaking work, clearing the land for crops and building another cabin for the Sparrows. However, both families were excited about their new lives in this new and fertile land. There was certainly more joy than sorrow—until the autumn of 1818.

"Aunt Nancy! Uncle Thomas! I don't know what it is. Something's wrong with Ma and Pa!" Nineteen-year-old Dennis came running into the Lincolns' cabin one beautiful October morning. His hands shook, and his usually rosy face was pale.

Without a word, Nancy jumped up to check on her sister and her brother-in-law. They were still living in the open-face shelter while the final touches to their cabin were being finished. Nancy knelt next to her sister on her bed of leaves.

"Betsy, tell me what hurts," Nancy said, reaching out to touch her sister's forehead. Both Betsy and Tom were burning up, nearly delirious with fever. They had been sick all night, and now just lay in the leaves, trembling and pressing their hands against the pain in their stomachs.

"Stomach. Like burning," was all Betsy could say. And then, "Doctor."

But the nearest doctor was fifty miles away. It would be days before he would be able to reach the homestead at Pigeon Creek. Betsy and Tom needed help right away.

For two days, Nancy Lincoln barely left the open-face shelter. But nothing she did seemed to help the Sparrows. On the third day, both Betsy and Tom died.

"It was God's will," Thomas Lincoln said again and again as he, Abe, and Dennis chopped down trees for the two coffins. He tried to comfort himself and the others with his calmness, but deep inside, he was terrified. Sickness was rarely understood and even more rarely treated with any kind of success. Thomas knew that a contagious disease could wipe out the entire family very quickly.

"Will we get sick too?" Abe asked his mother quietly the night after the Sparrows were buried. "Will we die?"

"No. We'll be fine," she said with a sad smile as she tucked him and Sarah into bed. "No one has gotten sick yet. I don't think it's something we can catch, or I would have already caught it."

The Lincolns and Dennis held their breath for nearly a week, waiting to see if they all would, in fact, be fine. Ten days passed, and life went on. A full harvest moon rose above the first crops one night, and though everyone was sad, hope began to return.

"Our prayers have been answered," Thomas Lincoln said at the dinner table that evening. But much later that night, he awoke to a strange sound. It was Nancy crying.

"My stomach," she said. "Like it's on fire."

Chapter 2

Too late, the warning spread across the small settlement of Pigeon Creek: *Don't drink milk from the cows that graze in the fields north of the creek.* These cows had been infected with what was simply known as "milk sickness," a deadly disease caused by eating a wild plant called "snakeroot." Drinking the milk from these cows had killed Tom and Betsy Sparrow. And now it was killing Nancy Lincoln. Nancy struggled to stay alive, to spend just a bit longer with her family, but she knew she was dying. Finally, before she lost the strength to speak, she called Abraham to her side.

"I am going away from you, Abraham," she said in nearly a whisper. "I shall not return. I know that you will be a good boy, that you will be kind to Sarah and to your father. I want you to live as I have taught you."

Nine-year-old Abraham held his mother's hand, but he forced back the tears. He didn't want his mother to see him crying. Nineteen-year-old Dennis, who had moved in with the Lincolns after his parents died, stood in the doorway. Years later, thinking back to that terrible time, he would write: "O Lord, I'll never forget the misery in that little log cabin in the woods when Nancy died. Abe was only somewhere around nine years old, but he never got over the miserable way his mother died."

It all seemed so sudden. In the space of only a few weeks, the little settlement of the Lincolns and the Sparrows went from secure and hopeful to dark and mournful. Gone were the sounds of Betsy and Nancy singing hymns as they spun yarn by the fire. Tom Sparrow's deep laughter and constant whistling were replaced by the lonesome late fall wind. It would be an exceptionally difficult winter. Thomas Lincoln, along with help from Abe, used logs that had been set aside to finish the Sparrows' cabin to make a third coffin in as many weeks. They laid Nancy Lincoln near a deer-run in the woods, a peaceful spot. Abe later recalled, "Deer were the only wild animals she wasn't afraid of."

In the year that followed, Abe, his father, and Dennis kept busy with the crops and the farm.

Their situation was hardest, perhaps, on eleven-year-old Sarah, who was often left alone all day to do the cooking, cleaning, mending, and care of the cabin. Try as she might, she could not even come close to replacing her mother. Before long, cobwebs hung in the corners of the cabin, and dirt blew through the bearskin door and formed little piles everywhere. Everyone's clothing began to look dirty and ragged. Worst of all, Sarah had not learned how to cook, so most of the meals were disasters. At night, Abe often heard his older sister crying herself to sleep. It was almost more than he could bear.

"Things will get better," Abe whispered across the loft where they slept.

After a long silence, Sarah answered, "I know. It's just . . . it's mostly that I'm lonesome here. You all have each other, but I'm here alone all day."

The next day, Abe was thinking of what his sister had said, when he and his father came across a baby raccoon that had somehow gotten separated from its mother. Even as a young boy, Abe couldn't stand seeing either people or animals afraid or in pain. He secretly tucked the little raccoon into his big coat pocket and fed it bits of biscuit all day. That evening, he pulled the small animal out of his pocket and handed it to Sarah.

"To keep you company," Abe said with a proud smile.

"Oh!" Sarah looked happier than Abe had seen her in a long time. The she lowered her voice. "But what about Pa? I don't think . . ."

They both looked over at their father who, as he had done nearly every evening since their mother had died, just sat staring blankly into the fireplace.

"He won't even notice," Abe said with a shrug.

The pet raccoon helped Sarah's spirits, but nothing much changed around the cabin. As the days got shorter and colder, life at Pigeon Creek became bleaker. There was rarely any laughter, and Thomas Lincoln's storytelling had all but disappeared. The cabin was in complete disarray, and no one even seemed to care anymore. Then, early one morning, Sarah and Abe woke to hear their father and Dennis talking outside the cabin. It sounded as though Dennis was upset, so Abe climbed down the pegs in the wall from the loft and stood near the bearskin door, listening.

"Won't be gone long," Thomas said.

"But why?" Dennis asked. "Winter's coming on, and I don't see why you'd want to *walk* all the way to Kentucky this time of year."

"Well, I can't take the horse. You all will need it. And I've got things that need taking care of in Kentucky. All the crops are in now, so it's time to go."

"But what for? It doesn't make sense."

"Don't matter what for!" Thomas Lincoln said, his voice rising sharply. "I'll be back soon enough."

Dennis looked at the ground, ashamed of making his uncle angry.

"Look here," Thomas said more gently. "You're the man of the house while I'm gone. Take care of things."

With that, the two shook hands, and Abe peeked through the bearskin to watch his father turn and walk down the dirt road, a huge sack over his shoulder. He ran outside to say goodbye, but Dennis grabbed him by the shoulder.

"It's best to let him go like that," Dennis said. "He didn't want to have to explain or have a lot of goodbyes. Says he'll be back soon."

That was in late November. By Christmas Eve, Thomas Lincoln had still not returned. Abe, Sarah, and Dennis huddled around the fire in filthy, ragged clothes, eating burned cornbread. Abe did his best to tell a few funny stories to make his sister laugh, but there was little joy in the cabin that night.

Another month passed. Then another. Abe began to wonder if his father had died too. What kind of business could possibly take three months?

Then one cool March afternoon, as Abe split logs for the fire, he heard the unusual sound of horses and a wagon coming up the dirt road. As the wagon got closer, Abe recognized his father driving it. Abe threw down his ax and ran toward the wagon, waving and shouting. But then he noticed that sitting next to his father was a pretty woman Abe had never seen before. And sitting behind them were three young people, two girls and a boy, all around his and Sarah's age. Abe then stopped and shyly watched the approaching wagon.

"Well, come on now!" Thomas Lincoln shouted in a happy voice that Abe hadn't heard since before his mother had died. "Abe, Sarah! Come and meet your new mother."

New mother? Abe and Sarah looked at each other and then back at the wagon. Already, the pretty woman was climbing down and rushing over to them.

"I've heard so much about both of you!" She leaned down, put her arms around both children, and hugged them tightly. "I'm so very happy to finally meet you," she said with a wide, genuine smile. Abraham looked into her eyes and smiled a bashful smile in return.

"I liked her immediately," Lincoln, as an adult, wrote years later. And, perhaps because she seemed to suddenly appear and rescue them from such horrible circumstances, Lincoln also wrote, "She was my angel mother."

Thomas Lincoln's new wife, Sally Bush Johnston, had been an old love of Thomas's, but she had ended up marrying a different man. By sad coincidence, Sally's husband had died from the flu about the same time that Nancy Lincoln had died from milk sickness. When Thomas received news of this death from a friend back in Elizabethtown, Kentucky, where Sally lived, he immediately set out to ask her to be his wife. There were many odds and ends and details to attend to before Sally could return with Thomas to Pigeon Creek, but she said yes to his marriage proposal.

Young Abe was overwhelmed by the huge wagon piled high with expensive furniture, fancy blankets, woven rugs, dishes, and even mirrors. As he stood staring at it, two young girls and a boy a few years older than himself came out from behind the wagon.

"Pleased to meet you," the boy said politely, holding out his hand. "I'm your new brother, John. And these here are my sisters, Elizabeth and Matilda. Now they're your sisters too." John smiled awkwardly and looked uncomfortable. Abe shuffled his feet and looked at the ground.

"You like to fish?" Abe finally asked.

"You bet," John said with a big, goofy grin. And from that point on, there was no more awkwardness between the two boys.

With the arrival of Sally, many changes came to the Lincoln household. New furniture made it look like a real home, and new beds with real feather comforters made it feel like one. All Abe had ever known was pine straw for a mattress and bearskins for blankets. Sally demanded a few real glass windows, wood plank floors instead of dirt, and a sturdy wooden door with a lock in place of the filthy bearskin that had hung in the doorway for years. She cleaned every inch of the cabin and made incredible meals of roast turkey, mashed potatoes, and even strawberry pie.

But perhaps the biggest change Sally insisted upon had nothing to do with the Lincoln home.

"Abe wants to learn, Thomas. He's an unusually curious boy. He should start school next week." Sally and Thomas were talking quietly in front of the fire after the children had gone to bed.

Thomas sighed. He had been through this before with Nancy, but this was different. Sally was not the kind of woman who would back down once she had her mind set.

"But he's not that bright, Sally. It takes him forever to learn anything," Thomas argued weakly.

"It may be true that he is not the quickest learner," Sally agreed, "but he is very bright. There's a difference."

(Of this point, Lincoln himself would one day write: "I am slow to learn and slow to forget that which I have learned. My mind is like a piece of steel—very hard to scratch anything on it, and almost impossible after you get it there to rub it out.")

And so Abe began going to school more regularly, though his learning was constantly interrupted by the work his father needed him to do. At 13, Abe was already nearly six feet tall and, though quite thin, he was exceedingly strong. Thomas Lincoln thought his son's size and strength were being wasted in a classroom. Furthermore, Thomas was bothered by what he viewed as his son's continual laziness. Abe would study the way smoke blew from chimneys, the patterns in which birds took flight, how vines grew around trees, or the way minnows moved against currents. Sometimes he would stand nearly motionless for an hour, watching something that interested him. It drove his father crazy.

One morning, Thomas decided that a new chore was more important than school. As Abe walked out with his one book and a lunch bag, Thomas handed him a shotgun.

"Time for you to learn how to hunt," Thomas said, expecting his son to be excited. But Abe just looked at the gun with a frown.

"Don't worry. You're a good shot," Thomas pointed out. "I've seen you practicing."

Abe knew his father was right. But shooting at targets and tree limbs was one thing. Shooting at animals was another. Abe and Thomas walked quietly along the edge of the woods for a mile or so until they spotted several turkeys feeding along a hillside. They crept closer.

"All right, Abe," Thomas whispered. "We're close enough. Take aim at the biggest one. You should be able to bring him down with no problem."

Abe looked through the shotgun's sight, but his hands were shaking, making it hard to focus his aim. He took a deep breath and felt a little sick. Then he pulled the trigger.

"Yes!" Thomas slapped his son on the back and jumped up to run over to the dead bird as the other turkeys took off in terrified, clumsy flight. Abe slowly walked over and looked at the turkey; it was still flapping a wing as it died. Although Abe understood that hunting was necessary to put food on the table, after that first day of hunting with his father, he could never bring himself to shoot another animal as long as he lived. "I am in favor of animal rights as well as human rights," Lincoln would say in a speech one day in the future. "That is the way of a whole human being."

A small crowd had gathered behind the grain mill in the little town of Pigeon Creek. Mostly young boys and men, they were doubled over laughing. One boy about Abe's age was laughing so hard that tears streamed down his face. In the middle of the group was tall, lanky Abe Lincoln, standing on a wooden crate.

"And so the righteous, I say the *righteous*, will find the path, *ahem!* to glory. TO GLORY, I say!" Abe shouted, all the while making quirky movements, blinking rapidly, and clearing his throat loudly. "Ahem. *Ahem*! Now then, let us turn, ahem, to Luke, chapter, *ahem*! 1, verse 30."

The group clapped and cheered as Abe took an exaggerated bow and stepped off the wooden crate. Many in the group followed Abe as he went to the front of the mill to pick up grain, and then to the general store to buy some material for Sally. Even as a teenager, Abe was quickly gaining a reputation as a funny storyteller and a bit of a joker, and people liked to be around him. But those who knew him well knew that he was equal parts shy boy and showoff. As calm and well-spoken as he could be telling a story to a group of twenty men, he often became tongue-tied and nervous around girls.

Later that day, Abe walked home with his arms full of goods from town, grinning to himself about his "performance" behind the grain mill. But when the cabin came into view, Abe's heart sank. Standing at the front door were Abe's father and the pastor of the church the Lincolns attended. Thomas Lincoln's arms were folded, and he was shaking his head as though disappointed about something. Abe had a pretty good idea what that "something" might be.

"Abe, Pastor Stevens has paid us a visit to talk about you," Thomas said sternly, glaring at Abe.

"About . . . about . . . me?" Abe repeated nervously.

"Yes, son," the pastor said. "I hear that you do a good imitation of me, right down to the way I blink my eyes and clear my throat."

Abe was mortified. He had never meant to hurt the pastor's feelings. He actually liked Pastor Stevens quite a lot; that was why he could imitate him so well.

"Yes sir," was all Abe could say as he stared at the ground.

"I hear that you can even draw a crowd of boys your own age to watch you repeat an entire sermon in my voice. Word's gotten back to me that some of those boys are planning to start coming to Sunday services just to see how well you imitate me."

Abe just hung his head.

"Don't worry," Thomas said to Pastor Stevens. "I'll give Abe a punishment he won't soon forget."

The pastor laughed out loud. "*Punishment*? Why, Mr. Lincoln, your son has a rare talent, an ability to draw people to listen to him. I certainly take no offense. That is probably the first time many of those boys have ever listened to an entire sermon. It will certainly be the first time they have ever come to church."

Pastor Stevens walked over and put his arm around Abe's shoulders.

"Son, you keep right on doing what you're doing. I just wanted to stop by and thank you. You have quite a gift. You may be a remarkable preacher one day."

With that, the pastor tipped his hat, got back on his horse, and rode off with a friendly wave goodbye. Thomas and Abe stood there in silence for a minute, watching him ride away. Finally, Thomas just scratched his head and took a long look at his son, who was now taller than he was. Abe was trying very hard not to smile.

"Well, if that don't just beat all," Thomas said as he headed back into the cabin.

Chapter 3

"Wait! Stop! What are you doing?"

Fifteen-year-old Abe Lincoln splashed across Pigeon Creek to a group of boys all kneeling by the riverbank. One of the boys held down a large turtle that was desperately trying to escape its captor and claw its way back to the water. An older boy kneeled nearby, holding a red-hot coal with a pair of small tongs. Abe was well aware of what the boys were getting ready to do. He had seen a turtle's shell burned through with a coal before, and it was a horror he had never forgotten. He could never understand why boys his age wanted to torture animals.

"Stop it!" Abe shouted, kicking water at the boys and on the coal. He bent over and pulled the turtle away, giving it a little push back into the creek.

"How would you like someone to do that to you?" Abe yelled, his dark eyes blazing with anger. Most of the boys knew Abe and liked him. They also knew how he felt about hurting animals, so they just stood silently, reluctant to say anything. But the older boy walked up to Abe.

"What are you gonna do about it? Don't look like you could do too much. You ain't nothing but skin and bones. Look like a scarecrow," he said with a sneer.

Abe didn't like to fight with his fists, but he hated to back down when he knew he was right. Given the chance, he preferred to fight with words first.

"I'll fight you if that's what you want," Abe said. "But think about this first. That turtle is one of God's creatures, just like we are. I don't suppose God made that creature so that one of His other creations could torture it to death."

The older boy couldn't think of an argument for this. And he felt just a little ashamed when he noticed several of the other boys nodding in agreement. In anger, he kicked the tongs and coal into the creek and walked away.

At 15, Abe was nearly six feet, four inches tall. And though he towered over nearly everyone, he was, as many people liked to describe him, thin as the rails he split with his axe. Still, he had incredible strength. Townspeople often asked Abe for a hand when something extremely heavy had to be lifted or moved. It was rumored that he could lift a 300-pound keg over his head.

But for all his strength and stature, Abe was an awkward boy. His shyness wasn't helped by the fact that, because he grew so fast, his jacket sleeves ended at his elbows and his pants legs showed about six inches of shin. On top of this, he had big ears that seemed to stick straight out; a long, sad face; and a head full of wild, unruly hair. As a grown man many years later, he would often joke about his looks. (Upon seeing a photograph of himself for the first time, he dryly commented, "It looks most horribly like me.") But as a teenager, standing out in a crowd, literally, was often embarrassing and difficult for Abe.

Even so, Abe took advantage of his height and strength whenever he could—particularly if it involved doing something funny. One morning in early spring, a neighbor came by with his five-year-old son. His wife was sick in bed back at their cabin.

"I'm wondering," the neighbor asked Sally Lincoln, "if my son, David, could stay here for the day while you come and care for my wife. I have seven acres of corn planting to tend to, and I just can't seem to manage everything."

It was common for neighbors to drop everything to care for one another, so Sally willingly agreed. She was right in the middle of spring cleaning, but caring for a sick neighbor was far more important.

"Abe, Sarah, look after David today. I'll be home to make you all dinner later this afternoon," Sally instructed.

Abe spent most of the day outside looking after and playing with David, while Sarah continued with the spring cleaning inside the cabin. One of the main chores was brushing "whitewash," a very thin, cheap kind of white paint, on the walls and ceiling to cover up all the wood-smoke stains from the winter.

As a storm cloud approached, Abe and little David headed back to the cabin. Abe looked down and noticed that both his and David's shoes were very muddy, so he took his shoes off just outside the cabin door and ordered David to do the same. But, suddenly, a mischievous grin spread over Abe's face.

"Wait a minute, Davy," Abe said. "On second thought, keep your shoes on. I have an idea that might get me in trouble, but it'll be worth it."

With that, Abe picked David up and carried him into the cabin. With his strong arms,

Abe lifted David high over his head upside-down so that David's feet reached the freshly whitewashed cabin ceiling.

"Okay, Davy—take a walk across the ceiling!" Abe carried Davy across the length of the cabin in this manner until footprints reached from one end of the ceiling to the other. It looked ridiculously funny. Even Sarah, who had helped Sally whitewash the ceiling, burst out laughing.

Later that afternoon, Sally returned from the neighbor's house, and David, barely containing his giggles, left with his father. Sarah and Abe sat quietly, their faces hidden behind books. For quite some time, Sally chatted away about her day and moved around the cabin, getting things ready for dinner. Then her chatter stopped abruptly. Abe peered carefully over his book and saw Sally staring at the ceiling.

"How on earth . . .?"

Unable to contain himself, Abe threw his book down and roared with laughter. Sarah laughed herself into hiccups. Sally tried to look angry, but ultimately broke down into laughter too. And Abe was perfectly happy to spend the rest of that evening cleaning the ceiling and re-painting it. Making everyone laugh had been worth it.

For all his joking, however, Abe was a serious and, quite often, very quiet teenager. Those who lived in Pigeon Creek were well acquainted with the sight of tall, thin Abe Lincoln in his too-short pants and jackets, with a somber expression on his face, walking slowly down the street while reading a book. Often, he was spotted just sitting with his chin in his hand, his brow wrinkled in thought. Sometimes he could sit like this for more than an hour. As always, Thomas Lincoln viewed his son's brooding thoughtfulness and love of reading as laziness.

"Look at him!" Thomas said angrily one morning, pointing to Abe, who was standing in a cornfield. Abe was leaning back against the plow horse, his book held up to catch the sunlight.

Sally smiled. Unlike Thomas, she loved to see Abe reading and learning, and she encouraged and challenged him to learn something new every day. "Oh, Thomas, calm down. He's just taking a break."

"Well, why can't he take a break like any normal boy and sit down, rest, or eat something? Always with a different book wasting his time. Laziness! That's all it is," Thomas grumbled.

In fact, Abe was rarely with a "different book." Books were incredibly difficult to come by in the little frontier village of Pigeon Creek, so Abe was usually re-reading a book he had already read a few times. His favorite books were *Aesop's Fables*, *Robinson Crusoe*, *Pilgrim's Progress*, and the Bible. These were the four books he owned, but if he heard about a book that someone was willing to lend him, Abe would often walk for miles to borrow it. As Abe's cousin Dennis recalled in his old age, "Seems to me I never saw Abe after he was 12 that he didn't have a book somewhere around. He'd put a book inside his shirt and go out to the field to plow. When noon came, he'd sit under a tree and read. And when he came home at night, he'd tilt a chair back by the chimney, put his feet on the rung, and sit on his backbone and read."

Abe was interested in the lives of past presidents, particularly in the life of George Washington, who had died only ten years before Abe was born. When Abe heard that a neighbor several miles away had a book titled *The Life of Washington*, he thought nothing of walking the seven-mile roundtrip to borrow it. Abe stayed awake half the night reading the book by candlelight. Finally, he tucked the book between two logs in the cabin wall so that he wouldn't forget to take it out to the fields the next morning, and he fell asleep.

Just before dawn, a heavy rainstorm poured down. Because the book was in the wall of the cabin, the cover became soaked. Upon awaking, Abe was mortified to see what had happened—he had ruined the book. Instead of working in the fields that day, Abe immediately walked to the home of the book's owner and explained what had happened. It would have been easy enough to make up a story about the book, but Abe always told the truth.

"I know I need to repay you, but I don't have any money," Abe said.

The farmer thought for a moment, looking at the gangly teenage boy with the long, serious face. "I'll tell you what," he said. "You work in my orchard picking apples for two days, and we'll call it even."

At the end of the second day, the man met Abe out in the orchard and handed him *The Life of Washington*. It had been dried out, and though it was not as good as new, it was in decent shape.

"It's yours, Abe. You've earned it," the farmer said with a smile. "I appreciate your honesty, and I'm sure Mr. Washington would too if he were still alive."

This famous incident, along with many more like it, would one day earn Lincoln the nickname "Honest Abe."

Those who remembered the teenaged Lincoln recalled that he, as often as not, seemed awkward and sad. He was always a polite and helpful boy, but he suffered from bouts of sadness that he found hard to shake. Today, his sadness might be traced to depression or to the sudden loss of his mother when he was so young. But back in 1825, people simply thought he was moody. To make matters worse, Abe's father punished him for being sad, often blaming his reading or studies. Slowly, Abe became distant toward his father. The father and son had no interests in common and quite often had strong disagreements. Thomas felt that life as a farmer and a carpenter should be good enough for his son; after all, it had been good enough for him. However, Abe wanted more. Much more.

As Abe grew into his late teens and his friends began dating (or, as it was called back then, "courting") girls, Abe hung back shyly. He still loved to tell stories, give funny speeches, and even imitate the pastor from time to time. Yet as soon as a girl his age showed up, he would stumble over words and lose his place. Perhaps he was self-conscious about his height or his poorly fitting clothes. However, even as a grown man, Lincoln would often comment on his awkwardness with women.

"A woman is the only thing I am afraid of that I know will not hurt me," he said one time. And another time: "Others have been made fools of by the girls, but this can never with truth be said of me. I, most definitely, make a fool of myself." Lincoln could joke about it years later, but as a teenager, it was definitely not a laughing matter.

When Abe was 17, his older sister, Sarah, got married. Abe had always been quite close to his sister, particularly after their mother had died. Now that Sarah was no longer around, Abe grew more and more restless, longing to leave the little settlement in Indiana and see some of the world he had read about in books. At the very least, Abe wanted to start earning some money doing something different from plowing a field or chopping wood.

Abe and his cousin, Dennis, worked together for a while, running a ferry boat up and down the Anderson River, a river not far from Pigeon Creek. It didn't show Abe much of the world, but he did earn six dollars a month, which seemed like a lot of money to Abe. Since he was not yet 21, he had to turn the money he earned over to his father, but Abe was just glad to be doing something different. Rivers and their navigation had always fascinated Abe.

When he could find them, he often read books about traveling the big rivers.

In his spare time, Abe built a small rowboat for personal use to carry him up and down the river from Pigeon Creek to his ferry job. One evening, as Abe was untying the rowboat to head home, two very well-dressed men carrying heavy trunks approached him.

"Ferry's done running?" one of the men asked.

"Yes sir," Abe replied, wondering where the men were headed and what they would do if they were stranded out here in the middle of nowhere.

"Well, we're in a fine mess," the other man said with a disgusted groan. "How on earth are we going to get three miles downriver?"

Without a word, Abe picked up the men's trunks and hauled them to his boat and then motioned for them to get in.

"Headed that way anyway," Abe explained. "It certainly will be no trouble to drop you wherever you're headed."

The two men jumped at the offer. Three miles later, as Abe hauled the men's trunks back out to the riverbank, the men tossed a silver half-dollar each into Abe's boat as payment. It was more money than Abe had ever made in a day. Forty years later, Lincoln recalled, "I could scarcely believe my eyes as I picked up the money. I could not believe that I, a poor boy, had earned a dollar in less than a day. The world seemed wider and fairer before me."

That "wider and fairer" world beyond Abe's little corner of Indiana was soon to become even more appealing. In 1828, Sarah died in childbirth. Abe was crushed by the passing of his sister. She had been only 21 years old, in fine health, and was looking forward to raising a family a few miles down the road from the Lincoln cabin. Although Abe was itching to see some of the world, he had definitely been excited about becoming an uncle and seeing his sister's children grow up. Now all of that was gone. And Abe was ready to go too.

"I need a strong young man to help my son navigate a flatboat down the Ohio and then the Mississippi to New Orleans," James Gentry, a businessman near Pigeon Creek, said to Abe one summer morning. A "flatboat" was basically just a large raft with a small cabin in the center. Flatboats were used to transport goods, often livestock and produce, along rivers to other cities. Nearly 3,000 flatboats a year made their way down the Mississippi in the 1820s.

"I'll do it," Abe said immediately. *New Orleans!* he thought excitedly. Abe had never seen a big city before. And he had certainly never traveled 1,200 miles before, the distance from Pigeon Creek to New Orleans by way of the Ohio and Mississippi Rivers.

"You sure?" Gentry asked Abe, eyeing him carefully. "It's not just floating along down a lazy river, son. The Ohio is gentle enough, but once you hit the Mississippi, you're on a monster of a river full of dangerous currents, hidden sandbars, and rocky crags."

Abe just nodded confidently.

"I can pay you only eight dollars a month plus your travel expenses," Gentry continued. "And it will likely be a trip of nearly two months."

"That all sounds fine to me," Abe said, still nodding.

Gentry sized Abe up. At 6 feet, 6 inches and only 170 pounds, Abe was a spidery young man. But Gentry knew Abe's physical strength. And he admired Abe's honesty.

"So you can handle the river?" Gentry asked.

"Yes sir," Abe replied.

"The backbreaking work?"

"Yes sir."

"The weeks and weeks away from home?"

"Yes sir."

"And how about . . ." Here, Gentry paused. "How about the river pirates?"

River pirates? Abe thought. But he wanted the adventure, the journey into the wider and fairer world.

"Yes sir, Mr. Gentry. There's nothing I can't handle."

Chapter 4

"The way I see it, if we can get past Cave-in-Rock, we should be able to make it the rest of the way without running into pirates," Abe said as he ran his finger along the dark line of the Ohio River. Abe and Mr. Gentry's son, Allen, leaned over a large map spread out on the deck of the flatboat. It was April 1828, and they were preparing to leave the next morning.

"Cave-in-Rock" was a fifty-foot cave at a bend in the Ohio River, and it was notorious for being a hideout for pirates. Most of these river pirates only wanted to steal the cargo of the flatboats, but others, like the Mason Gang, often killed the pilots of the flatboats—sometimes just for fun. Abe and Allen studied the map and plotted how they would keep to the far side of the cave when they passed by.

They also studied the sharp and dangerous turns of the rivers and the places where rocks jutted out of the riverbanks. Mr. Gentry had been right; this would be no easy float for fun.

Abe worked long days on the river for those next two months. Up at sunrise, he would take the long pole that helped steer the flatboat and push it into the riverbed over and over again. On a good day, the boat moved at a rate of four to six miles an hour. At the end of the day, Abe and Allen would tie the flatboat to a tree along the edge of the river. Sometimes as the sun was setting, Abe would stare with amazement at the massive steamboats that occasionally passed by. On their decks stood men and women in elegant evening dress. Sometimes Abe would wave at these rich passengers, but they rarely waved back. As the daylight faded, Abe and Allen would head off to sleep in the little cabin in the middle of the flatboat, surrounded by sacks of grain, barrels of salted pork, and even live pigs.

Weeks passed, and it looked as though Abe and Allen would make it to New Orleans safely. Cave-in-Rock had passed by quietly. And now the two young men had gotten as far as Baton Rouge. It was a rainy, moonless night as Abe drifted off, listening to the waters of the Mississippi lapping against the shore where they had tied their boat. Suddenly, the sound of footsteps shocked Abe and Allen wide awake.

"Somebody's on the boat," Abe whispered, grabbing a huge wood club, the only weapon onboard.

"Voices," Allen said quietly to Abe. "I can make out more than three or four. We're in trouble."

"Pirates?" Abe asked. He thought they'd be past that threat by now.

"We'll see," Allen whispered back. "Let's surprise them." Allen grabbed another club, and the two men crept to the doorway of the cabin and peeked out. In the gloomy night, they could barely make out six or seven men moving around the deck. They were picking up sacks of grain and trying to roll the barrels of pork.

"On the count of three," Abe whispered. "One . . . two . . . THREE!"

Abe and Allen burst through the door of the cabin. Abe's height and strength gave him a big advantage, and he crashed through the pirates, his wooden club smashing the sacks out of their hands. One of the pirates cracked a heavy stick against Abe's forehead and left a scar that Abe would carry with him for the rest of his life. It was seven men against two, but Abe and Allen fought with such ferocity that the pirates finally gave up and ran off with only one sack of grain.

"Those were all black men," Allen said, once he and Abe had caught their breath. "I never thought of river pirates as being black."

"Well," Abe said after a moment's thought, "I suppose both black and white men are capable of the same good and bad. There's no difference."

"That's right. Come on up and look at his teeth. Check his muscles. Make sure you're satisfied before you make your bid. This is Ben. Strong young Negro. You'll get years of hard work from him." A fat, sweating auctioneer, with the stub of a cigar between his teeth and a whip in his hand, shouted out to a crowd of potential buyers along a New Orleans dock on the Mississippi.

"All right, boy," he barked at Ben, "walk around in a circle now. Show 'em you ain't got anything wrong with your legs." The auctioneer lifted the whip slightly to let Ben know he'd better do as he was told. Ben looked at no one, keeping his head low, but every now and then he would cast a desperate glance at a young black woman who was grouped with other black women on the far side of the dock. She tried to smile at Ben, but tears were pouring down her face.

Abe and Allen stood behind the crowd of buyers. An expression of shock and anger slowly crept across Abe's face. While he had seen slaves before, he had never seen them sold.

"That's a man!" Abe said quietly to Allen. "Why, they treat him like he's no more than a cow or a pig."

Allen nodded. "And the woman he keeps looking at—that's likely his wife. Unless the buyer wants a woman in the bargain, they'll be separated forever. The same goes for children. Entire families are usually split up among the highest bidders."

"But that's *wrong*," Abe said, struggling to keep his voice down. "It's cruel."

The auctioneer was now welcoming the group of men who had come forward to prod Ben's muscles, open his mouth and inspect his teeth, and make him walk back and forth. One man even checked through his hair for fleas and then gave Ben a hard kick to see how tough he was. Abe turned away in disgust; he had seen enough. As he and Allen walked through the streets of New Orleans, Abe saw dozens of sights he'd never seen before: drunken sailors, dancing girls, vendors with strange and exotic foods, musicians on busy street corners. But many years later, the memory that would stand out from that first trip into the wider world would be the memory of the horrible injustice of that slave auction.

"I am naturally anti-slavery," Lincoln would one day conclude. "If slavery is not wrong, nothing is wrong."

When Abe returned from the trip to New Orleans, he had a dream of becoming the captain of a steamboat. The massive steamboats, filled with elegant people, had fascinated him. However, Abe quickly discovered that two months of poling a flatboat didn't exactly qualify him to captain a steamboat. So he returned to doing odd jobs around Pigeon Creek and helping out at home. At 19, Abe was still obligated by law to give all his earnings to his father for nearly two more years. Often, fathers allowed their sons to go out into the world at 18 or even younger, but Thomas Lincoln would not give permission to Abe.

Abe was, understandably, often frustrated with being in the situation he was in. He and his father no longer got along well at all. Abe felt his father was simply using him for work as long as he could. Abe continued to read about the world around him, but now even his reading irritated him. It didn't seem fair that so much was out there waiting to be discovered while he was forced to plow fields and feed chickens. His stepmother, Sally, understood Abe's frustration and did her best to keep his spirits up. Though Abe was distant with his own father, he was remarkably close to Sally, continuing to refer to her as an "angel" throughout his life.

Finally, Abe turned 21. But as fate would have it, almost immediately after Abe's birthday, Thomas Lincoln decided to move the family to Illinois, where farmland was better and cheaper. Although Abe was legally free to leave, and certainly wanted to, he felt obligated to help with the move. When the family arrived, Abe once again found himself helping his father build a new cabin. Abe's plan was to take off as soon as the cabin was finished in the late fall, but, again, fate had other plans in store. The winter of 1830 in Illinois went down in history as one of the worst ever. It became known as the winter of the "Deep Snow," and blizzards buried farmlands and homes. Temperatures rarely got above zero for nearly two months, and thousands of people, including Abe, were literally trapped in their cabins.

Abe spent that winter waiting for it to end, staring out the cabin window at the endlessly falling snow. When springtime came, nothing, not even fate, was going to hold him back. He was ready to strike out on his own.

"*Abraham.* Abraham Lincoln." Lincoln reached out to shake hands with a merchant named Denton Offutt. Lincoln was now a man, and he no longer wanted to be called "Abe." As he had often told his stepmother, he had always hated the nickname, but it was nearly impossible to change what people had always called him ever since he was a child.

But Lincoln had now arrived in a new town, ready for a new start. People would call him either "Abraham" or "Lincoln." The town, New Salem, Illinois, seemed large to Lincoln, though it probably had only about 150 people in it. Still, this was much bigger than Pigeon Creek. And one of the first people Lincoln met was Offutt, a short, good-natured man who was looking for a younger man to help him with his new store.

Offutt had a new general store in New Salem that sold everything from postage stamps to whiskey. He had a bit of a reputation for drinking as much whiskey as he sold, but Lincoln liked the talkative, smiling Offutt right away.

"Looks like you might be better suited to some kinda work other than sitting behind a store counter," Offutt said, looking up at Lincoln towering nearly a foot above him.

"I'm happy to do any kind of work, Mr. Offutt," Lincoln said. "Behind a counter, chopping logs, steering a flatboat, or building a cabin. As long as I'm busy, I'm happy."

And so Offutt hired Lincoln to run the counter. It suited Lincoln because he had plenty of time to read, and it suited Offutt because it gave him plenty of time to "check" the whiskey inventory in the back room. Of greater importance for Lincoln, though, was the fact that he eventually met everyone in New Salem by working in one of the few stores in town. At first, people didn't know what to make of this odd-looking giant of a man in high-water pants. But they discovered soon enough that Lincoln was a kind, smart, and very funny man. Lincoln had learned quite early in life that the ability to make people laugh was one of the best ways to make new friends. And while he was past the age of imitating preachers, Lincoln could often draw a crowd in the little general store when he told a funny story.

One afternoon, Offutt watched a small crowd gather in his store, and he got an idea.

"You ever wrestle much?" Offutt asked Lincoln after everyone had left.

"Not if I don't have to," Lincoln said with a smile.

"But I bet you're pretty strong, right?"

"Sure," Lincoln said carefully. He had an idea of what his boss was up to. "I'm usually about the strongest fellow around. But I prefer to use it for work, not fighting."

"Hmm. Really. You don't say?" Offutt said absent-mindedly as he tipped his hat and headed out the door.

Within a few days, the men of New Salem were placing bets on a fight between Abraham Lincoln and Jack Armstrong. Armstrong was known as the toughest man in town, and no one had ever beaten him in a fight or wrestling match. Offutt had "accidentally" mentioned all around town that Lincoln could easily whip Armstrong in a wrestling match. Before Lincoln could say no to it, Armstrong was already boasting about how no scrawny beanpole was going to beat *him*. Lincoln had to go ahead with the match for the sake of his reputation.

A large circle of townspeople formed outside of Offutt's store on the morning of the match. Armstrong brought along his gang—a group of tough young men like himself. No one messed with the Armstrong gang. They were well known throughout the area for getting what they wanted, regardless of how they got it. Jack Armstrong sized Lincoln up and sneered. *He's all skin and bones*, Armstrong thought. *I'll bet he can't get one hold on me.*

But Armstrong was wrong. From the start, Lincoln had the upper hand. He may not have been as tough as Armstrong, but he was stronger and far more calm and collected. Lincoln thought the match out, while Armstrong jumped into it like a wildcat. When Armstrong realized he was in danger of losing the match, he suddenly made an unfair move in an attempt to trip Lincoln. The crowd booed as Lincoln stumbled and Armstrong jumped on him. But just as quickly, Lincoln regained his balance and wrapped Armstrong up in a hold from which he couldn't free himself. The match was over. The crowd cheered, but Armstrong's gang was a group of sore losers. They ran toward Lincoln, shouting threats and retaliation. Lincoln sprang up and put his fists out.

"I'll fight every one of you, if that's what you want," he snarled angrily.

"Hold it there!" Jack Armstrong yelled to his gang. He turned to Lincoln and put out his hand to shake. "You won it fair and square, Lincoln," Armstrong admitted. "We could use a fighter like you in our group. You sure know the moves."

Lincoln shook Armstrong's hand and said, "I'd be glad to be friends, but I'm not much for fighting, if it's all the same to you."

Armstrong just smiled and shook his head in amazement. He'd never met such a gentle giant before. "All right, then. Friends it is."

And from that day on, Lincoln was always respected and treated as a friend by Jack Armstrong and his gang.

After the Armstrong fight, everyone in New Salem tried to get to know this unusual young man, Abraham Lincoln, better. Some did so by challenging him to foot races or wood-chopping contests. Lincoln rarely lost, but he remained humble and never bragged about his abilities. On the contrary, he often seemed embarrassed by the attention his natural strength brought him. Flaunting the fact that he could beat others was not in his nature.

However, some people were more interested in Lincoln's mind. One of these people was Mentor Graham, the local schoolteacher. Graham noticed that Lincoln was a dynamic and moving speaker. People loved to listen to Lincoln talk, and Lincoln loved standing up on a tree stump and giving speeches about anything from growing good corn to state politics.

"Interesting speech," Graham said to Lincoln one evening after Lincoln had just spoken about why he felt the local interest rates on loans were unfair. "Can I offer a suggestion that might make you an even better speaker?"

"Definitely!" Lincoln replied. Having never received much education, he was always eager to learn more, particularly when the offer came from a teacher.

"Let me give you some books on grammar and writing," Graham said. "Speaking and writing correctly are important if you want to be taken seriously. You're a good speaker, but a little learning will make you a great one. Important people are starting to take notice of you, Abraham."

Lincoln raised an eyebrow. "Taking notice of me? What do you mean?"

"Well," Graham said, rubbing his chin thoughtfully, "let me ask you this. Are you familiar with what a state legislator does?"

Lincoln had read many books about politics and politicians. He knew quite well that legislators helped form the laws that govern the states. In fact, in the speech he had just given, he had mentioned several times that Illinois state laws needed to be changed in order to be fairer to the people.

"Yes sir, I know exactly what a legislator does. But why do you ask?"

"There's been talk around town, son," Graham said. "There are those that want you to run for the legislature this fall. We need a young, smart man like you to represent our town and this area—a man who can move people with his words. What do you think of that?"

Lincoln was stunned at first. Only two years ago, he had been pushing a flatboat down the Mississippi. Now there was talk of his becoming a state legislator. Lincoln glanced down at his shin-high pants and his ragged jacket. In his typical dry fashion, he looked at Graham with a twinkle in his eye and said, "Well, I think I'd better get a new suit."

Chapter 5

"Land cannot be sold! The Great Spirit gave it to his children to live upon. So long as they live on it and cultivate it, they have the right to the soil. Nothing can be *sold* except things that can be carried away."

These were the words of the proud and fierce chief of the Sac and Fox Indian tribes. He was called "Black Hawk," and in the spring of 1832, he was furious with the United States government for forcing him and his tribes off the fertile Illinois farmlands that the Sac and Fox had lived on for centuries. Like Black Hawk, many Indians did not believe that land was something that could change hands by way of payment. They felt spiritually connected to the land in much the same way people feel connected to other people. The loved the land.

The idea of selling it was as horrible to them as the idea of selling people was to Lincoln.

For this reason, Chief Black Hawk gathered nearly 2,000 Indian warriors and began a march back to the Illinois lands that they felt had been stolen from them. In particular, Black Hawk and his warriors wanted to plant their traditional spring wheat in an area they called "Saukenuk." Saukenuk was considered a sacred territory to the Indians since many Indians had been buried in this area. To add insult to injury, however, the U.S. Army had built a military fort right in the middle of Saukenuk and renamed it "Rock Island."

The tribes had been told by the U.S. government to stay west of the Mississippi in areas designated for Indians to live. These areas were not nearly as good for planting crops, and the land was not considered as valuable as the land taken from the Indians. Still, most Indians moved to the new lands without a revolt—not Black Hawk, though. When word got out that Black Hawk and his warriors had crossed the Mississippi River and were headed to Illinois to reclaim their land, people were filled with fear and horror. Before long, gruesome reports of settlers in small northern Illinois settlements being tomahawked and scalped reached the Illinois governor. Immediately, he ordered troops to be formed all across Illinois to go to the aid of the settlements being attacked.

Down in New Salem, Lincoln was just beginning to work on his campaign for the state legislature when his plans were interrupted.

"Lincoln!"

"That's right—he's the one. Couldn't pick a better man."

"Abraham's a natural leader. He'll do it."

Outside the general store, a large crowd had gathered. A number of men, including Lincoln, had volunteered to fight in what was now being called the Black Hawk War. The New Salem volunteers would need a leader, and Lincoln was quickly elected. The group was primarily made up of the young, tough men from Jack Armstrong's gang, who had grown to admire and respect Lincoln greatly. Lincoln accepted his position as leader and designated Jack Armstrong as his first sergeant.

As it turned out, Lincoln and his company never saw any fighting action in the war, which was probably just as well as far as Lincoln was concerned. They did, however, have to assist in the burying of men after one particularly vicious battle. Some years later, Lincoln thought back to that horrible day and wrote:

> **The red light of the morning sun was streaming upon them as they lay with**

> **their heads toward us on the ground. And every man had a round, red spot on the top of his head, about as big as a silver dollar, where the Indians had taken his scalp. It was frightful, it was grotesque, and the red sunlight seemed to paint everything all over.**

However, Lincoln did have some sympathy for the Indians, in spite of having to witness their gruesome form of killing. Perhaps Lincoln could not fully understand the Indians' deep connection to the earth, but he understood that they, too, were men and women who felt the same pain, fear, and anger as anyone else.

Most of the men in Lincoln's company, though, barely saw the Indians as human.

"Kill him! Let's hang him from that tall oak tree," one of the men in Lincoln's command shouted as a terrified elderly Indian was led into the camp, surrounded by several of Armstrong's gang, who jabbed him with gun barrels and sticks.

"Hell, just shoot him and throw him in the river," another shouted.

The Indian, looking desperately from one face to another, held out a slip of paper. In his shaking hand was a document from U.S. authorities explaining that he was not from an enemy tribe and should not be harmed. But the boys from Armstrong's gang still wanted to kill him. They had been eager for some fighting since they arrived at the camp, and now their patience was running out. One of the boys began to drag the old man toward the hanging tree.

"Stop!" Suddenly Lincoln appeared in the middle of the commotion. He reached down and quickly read the document, and then looked up, his eyes furious.

"Let go of this man. We have no right to hold him, much less hurt him," Lincoln said.

"*Let him go?*" one of the younger soldiers in the company yelled. "What? Are you afraid of some old redskin?"

Lincoln walked right up to the young man and looked him in the eye. "If you want to fight someone so badly, fight me."

The young man looked away and muttered, "You're twice my size."

"Then choose your weapon," Lincoln said calmly, never breaking his steely gaze at the man.

Lincoln's company of men stood quietly. Finally, the young soldier just shrugged his shoulders and shook his head. Lincoln turned to the old Indian and helped him up, indicating that he was free to go. The men in Lincoln's company were angry about Lincoln's actions at the time, but years later, one soldier recalled, "As years went on and we looked back, we knew Mr. Lincoln was right. And we loved him for it."

When Lincoln returned home after the Black Hawk War, he joked about how little action he and his company had seen. He claimed that the only bloodshed he encountered was from killing mosquitoes, and the only hardship he experienced was having a poor company cook who fixed meals that tasted "like an old shoe." But Lincoln was quite serious about getting back to work on his campaign for the legislature. Twenty-three-year-old Lincoln had only a handful of weeks to travel around Illinois, making speeches. And while the people he met and spoke to liked him, he simply didn't have enough time. Lincoln lost his first election.

Back in New Salem, Offutt's store was not doing well, so he closed it and left town with barely a goodbye to anyone. Suddenly, Lincoln was jobless. Not one to sit around wasting time or feeling sorry for himself, Lincoln scrambled for work and, over the next two years, became something of a jack-of-all-trades. Some of his various jobs were successful; others were not.

Perhaps Lincoln's biggest failure was co-owning a store. He went into business with a friend that he didn't really know very well. To make matters worse, the town of New Salem was slowly getting smaller and smaller. People wanted to live near a big river, a main road, or a train route. Years earlier, when the town had been founded, being close to transportation was not a concern. But the United States was growing rapidly, and now people were restless and wanted to be on the move. As a result, many of the businesses in New Salem began failing, and one of them was Lincoln's store. He was left owing $1,100 (a *huge* sum in 1824!) on the business. He jokingly referred to this as "the national debt," but he worked exceedingly hard for many years to pay off every cent.

Next, Lincoln worked as the postmaster of New Salem. He had always enjoyed walking, and now his assignment as postmaster gave him plenty of opportunities to walk for miles and miles. Around this time, Lincoln began wearing his trademark top hat, the tall black hat that he is often shown wearing in photographs and paintings. Not being a person particularly concerned about fashion, Lincoln began wearing this style of hat for another reason altogether. He discovered that the roomy hat was perfect for carrying letters, leaving his hands free to hold a book and read as he walked. Before long, the people of New Salem grew used to seeing Lincoln delivering their mail from his hat.

To add to his income—delivering mail paid only two dollars a month—Lincoln split rails and did any odd jobs the people of New Salem gave him. He also taught himself how to be a land surveyor when a friend who had served under him in the Black Hawk War offered him this job. Surveying involved traveling by horseback and measuring plots of land for new settlers. As Lincoln rode through the miles of Illinois countryside, he often wrote poetry, read Shakespeare, or worked through complicated math problems in his head. Always, he was thinking, learning, and creating.

But none of these jobs gave Lincoln any sense of real satisfaction. After his first taste of running for office two years earlier, Lincoln longed to become involved in politics. He was not a vain man, but he was well enough aware of his talent for speaking to realize that maybe he could make a difference. And there were things Lincoln wanted to help change: tax laws, river traffic, and, most importantly, slavery. Most of the people in the Illinois legislature were from the southern part of the state, and they opposed "abolition," the ending of slavery. Lincoln became determined to win a legislative seat so that he could speak against slavery and work to bring about change.

In 1834, Lincoln attended every picnic, party, dance, and even quilting bee that he could find. He talked to everyone, gave speeches whenever he had the chance, and continued to study politics. Although his past two years of odd jobs had not been particularly satisfying, they had introduced him to hundreds of people. In the summer of 1834, many of these people voted for him. At only 25, he became a member of the Illinois state legislature.

"And *now* I really do need a suit," Lincoln pointed out to a friend. "But I can't afford one yet. Maybe in a few months or so."

The friend, a wealthy businessman, took a long look at Lincoln's ragged appearance and shook his head in laughter.

"For heaven's sake, Abraham, you can't walk into the legislature looking like that. They'll toss you out. Let me lend you the money. A man in your position needs to look the part of a gentleman."

And so Lincoln bought his first fancy suit for work. But looking the part of a gentleman would still have to wait a bit. On his way to his first day at the state capital, Lincoln heard crying and snorting coming from the side of the road. Looking down from his wagon, he saw a young pig that had gotten trapped in a pool of muddy water.

Oh no, Lincoln thought to himself, knowing his soft spot for animals. *Absolutely not. I cannot stop for a pig.* Lincoln rode on a bit further, but the cries of the animal followed him. Finally he stopped and sighed deeply, shaking his head. Then he pulled the wagon to the side of the road and walked back to the pig.

"Why, of all days, did you have to get stuck in the mud today?" Lincoln muttered at the pig as he leaned down to free it. Of course, in the process, Lincoln's suit was splattered with mud and water. Later that morning, as Lincoln entered the capital for the first time, all heads turned to stare at this strange-looking man in a top hat and a muddy suit.

"Good morning, gentlemen!" Lincoln said enthusiastically, as though there was nothing unusual about his appearance. "Beautiful day, isn't it?"

Thus began Abraham Lincoln's political career.

Lincoln's first years in the legislature were mostly a learning process. And one of the things he learned right away was that some of the older, well-educated politicians looked down on the fact that Lincoln had no real education. Certainly, Lincoln had read many books, but he'd never gone to school, much less college.

As a result, some of the legislators ignored his opinions and his speeches. They also knew that his past "professions" had consisted mostly of chopping wood, delivering letters, and building cabins. They felt that a man as uneducated and inexperienced as Lincoln should not be in the legislature at all. But another young politician, John Todd Stuart, saw that there was a great deal of promise in Lincoln. Stuart was a college-educated lawyer from Springfield, Illinois, and right away he was impressed by Lincoln's ability to think clearly and logically and, in turn, speak impressively. Stuart approached Lincoln one afternoon.

"You should become a lawyer," Stuart said.

Lincoln looked carefully at Stuart to see if he was joking. He wasn't.

"A lawyer?" Lincoln said with a grin. "I've never studied law, and as you may have heard a dozen times or more, I've never even been to school."

"I can help you learn everything you would need to know," Stuart continued. "Let me bring you some books next time we meet. I'll be glad to answer any questions along the way."

Of course, Lincoln readily agreed to this. So, in addition to learning the ropes of being a new legislator, and continuing to chop wood and deliver mail (even being a legislator didn't pay enough to live on), Lincoln studied hard to learn the law. Often, he would read late into the night, his long back bent over books spread out on a table, as dim candlelight flickered. Some of Lincoln's friends in New Salem worried about him, feeling that "he would craze himself" with so much work and study.

However, it was not all work and no play for Lincoln.

"She was a beautiful girl—as bright as she was beautiful. Sweet and angelic, she was loved by all who knew her." This was how the people of New Salem remembered a young girl named Ann Rutledge. Ann was the daughter of the owner of the Rutledge Tavern, where Lincoln lived. (Back then, "tavern" was the name given to boarding houses where young, unmarried men usually rented rooms.) Ann was an unusual girl in many ways. She was the only girl to have ever attended the local school through all the grades. Though she was soft-spoken, she was known to be an excellent storyteller—something that was typically considered a male talent.

Twenty-six-year-old Lincoln was still painfully shy around women his age. The older, married women of New Salem took pity on this poor, awkward bachelor and tried in vain to be matchmakers. But Lincoln seemed uninterested in, or downright afraid of, all the eligible young women in New Salem—except Ann Rutledge. Lincoln had met Ann when he first moved to New Salem and had always felt comfortable around her. This may have been because Ann was engaged to a local merchant named John McNamar, and, as a result, she was not threatening to Lincoln. After all, he couldn't fall in love with her; she was already taken. But Lincoln did fall in love.

In 1833, McNamar had left New Salem to attend to personal business in New York, promising to marry Ann as soon as he returned. While McNamar was gone, Ann and Abraham began spending more time together. They took long walks in the country, discussing ideas, books, and things that made both of them laugh. Ann began to think of Lincoln as one of her closest friends. Because Lincoln still worked as part-time postmaster for New Salem, he was able to see when letters arrived for Ann from John or when she sent letters back to him. For quite a while, letters went back and forth every few days. And then, suddenly, letters from John stopped coming.

"But he said he was returning to New York to take care of his father," Ann said to Lincoln during one of their walks. "I don't understand why he would suddenly just stop writing."

Lincoln was silent. It had now been two months since Ann had heard from John, and the town of New Salem had begun to gossip about it. In 1834, when a woman was abandoned by her fiancé, *she* was looked upon as being the cause of the breakup. Often, townspeople would assume that the woman had done something morally wrong. Lincoln, of course, thought no such thing. But he worried about what people might think of his friendship with Ann.

"Abraham, be honest with me," Ann said, stopping and looking into Lincoln's eyes. "Do you think he's coming back?"

A thousand thoughts went through Lincoln's head. All his old fears of dating and falling in love threatened to overwhelm him. Should he tell Ann how he felt? He sensed that she might feel the same about him, but what if she didn't? What if . . .

Finally, Lincoln looked back at Ann and simply spoke honestly. "No, Annie, I don't think he is."

Chapter 6

What was the real relationship between Lincoln and Ann Rutledge? The answer to that question has been debated for more than 170 years. Some people believe that the two were only close friends, since in all of Lincoln's writings and collected letters, there are barely any mentions of Ann and no letters written to her. But many other people believe that Lincoln simply felt he had to keep his relationship with Ann a secret. After all, even though McNamar had disappeared, he and Ann were still engaged. Proper behavior back then insisted that an engagement must be honored for at least a year, regardless of the circumstances.

Accounts by residents of New Salem during that time vary. Ann's cousin said that Ann and Lincoln wanted "to wait a year for their marriage after their engagement" until Lincoln was finished studying law. This, then, suggests that they were engaged. But Ann's own father always denied that his daughter and Lincoln were ever more than friends. Whatever the real story may have been, no one denied, as the winter of 1835 turned to spring, that the two were often seen together and were nearly inseparable.

Then came the summer of 1835. Incredible heat settled throughout the Midwest, and with the heat, day after day of rain. Large ponds and puddles of stagnant water gathered in all the little farming towns and settlements. Slowly, this dangerous water seeped into the well water that people drank. Before long, household after household contracted what, in those days, was called "brain fever." It was probably typhoid, a deadly disease spread by contaminated water. In the Rutledge house, several family members became ill—including Ann. Lincoln, risking his own health, cared for Ann, but she died very quickly.

Following Ann's death, Lincoln entered a dark time of deep sadness and depression. Already thin, he lost weight. He rarely slept. Townspeople watched Lincoln walk slowly to the cemetery nearly every day; he often spoke of how he could not bear to think of rain or snow falling on her grave. This was the third great loss Lincoln had endured. Indeed, the three deaths—of his mother, when he was just a boy; of his sister, to whom he was so close; and now of his first real love—may have made him bitter toward love and even toward himself. Not long after Ann's death, he wrote to a friend: "I have now come to the conclusion never to think of marrying, and for this reason: I can never be satisfied with anyone who would be blockhead enough to have me."

But life went on. Thankfully, Lincoln was re-elected to another two-year term in the Illinois legislature. The state capital had moved to Springfield, so, at a time when he probably needed a new start in a new town, Lincoln decided to move to Springfield as well. He had passed all his law exams, and John Todd Stuart, who had helped and encouraged Lincoln through all of the studying, was now offering Lincoln a job as a lawyer in his Springfield law firm. Slowly, the haze of depression began to lift from Abraham Lincoln.

Springfield in 1835 was a busy town of more than 2,000 people. Compared to New Salem or Pigeon Creek, it seemed like a big city to Lincoln. Lincoln rode into town on his horse, his only other belongings hanging from the saddle in two big sacks, and his dusty top hat drawing attention from all the passersby. Along the busy street were saloons, hotels, cafes, and even a theater where townspeople went to hear speeches. *A theater for speeches!* Lincoln thought. *That's a far cry from a tree stump or the general store.*

And perhaps because it was the one kind of place that seemed familiar to him, Abraham stopped at a general store. The owner, a young man with a handsome face and a wide smile, came out to greet Lincoln.

"What can I do for you today?" the owner asked.

"Well," Lincoln said slowly, looking around, "I'm new to town. I don't know quite yet what I'll need, but . . ."

"Welcome then! My name's Joshua Speed." Speed reached out and shook Lincoln's hand. "Where will you be living?"

Lincoln paused, somewhat embarrassed. "That's a good question, Mr. Speed. You see, my finances are such that I'm not certain I can afford a room here in Springfield—and yet, here I am."

Speed looked carefully at Lincoln. Years later, he would recall, "I never saw a sadder face." And something about Lincoln's sadness touched Speed.

"I'll tell you what," Speed replied. "I have a room I would be glad to share with you."

In the 1800s, sharing rooms and even beds was very common. Housing was extremely limited in frontier areas such as Springfield, so Lincoln did not find it odd that a bachelor storekeeper might offer to share his room. On the contrary, Lincoln was very pleased.

"What part of town might this room be in?" Lincoln asked.

Speed laughed out loud. "Why, sir, it's right up these stairs," he said pointing to a long staircase that led above the store.

Lincoln ran up the stairs, his long legs covering three steps at a time. Within a minute he ran back down the stairs with a bright smile replacing his sadness.

"Well, Speed, it looks good to me," he said sincerely. "I'll take it."

And that first meeting led to one of the strongest and longest-lasting friendships Abraham Lincoln ever had.

During the early 1800s, the two political parties in the United States were the Whigs and the Democrats. The Democrats tended to include what, today, we call "blue-collar" workers: farmers, laborers, and those who built or crafted items (anything from horseshoes to houses). These people were often suspicious of the government, preferring to run their own lives rather than having others tell them what to do. They liked the old way of life and didn't always support industry and growth. When it came to slavery, Democrats in the North usually opposed it, while Southern democrats supported it.

On the other side were the Whigs. Whigs included businessmen, doctors, and lawyers, who were excited about progress in the United States. The Whigs supported building highways and railroads, and they were willing to pay taxes to fund this growth. And Whigs were mostly against slavery. Some fought actively against slavery; they were known as "abolitionists" because they wanted to abolish slavery. They weren't against using force or fear tactics. Other Whigs were more moderate, hoping to change the minds of slave owners through talk and education. Lincoln was a moderate Whig.

Nearly every evening at Joshua Speed's general store, men would gather around the fireplace and talk. Often they told jokes or stories, and before long, as in New Salem, Lincoln became one of the favorites. He was different from the others in this group of men in a number of ways. First, though he enjoyed company, he rarely made close friends. He kept to himself, and, unless he was telling a story, he was quiet and thoughtful. Second, he never smoked or drank. Nearly all the men that gathered at Speed's had a drink or two, but not Lincoln. He was not against drinking for moral reasons; he just felt that a man could think and speak more clearly without it. And, third, Lincoln rarely got angry or raised his voice when debating political issues. This was not so with some of the other men, particularly the abolitionists.

"It needs to be crushed! Slavery should be destroyed. And slave holders should be imprisoned and their slaves set free," an older man said loudly one evening at Speed's.

"How exactly do you propose to do that?" Lincoln asked coolly.

"Force," the man replied. "I'd have no problem with sending the U.S. Army down to some of those Southern plantations and forcing those monsters to stop buying slaves."

"So," Lincoln continued calmly, "you're suggesting that we use government force to make people give up something that is still protected by the United States Constitution?"

The older man's eyes looked like they might pop out of his head. "*What?* What the hell are you talking about, Lincoln? Are you supporting slavery or what?"

"Of course not," Lincoln responded. "I'm supporting our Constitution. Perhaps you've forgotten that the original authors of the Constitution were slaveholders. There are laws and guidelines for owning slaves written into one of our country's most important legal documents."

The room of men was silent for a moment, all of them thinking about this.

"Look," Lincoln continued, "making changes takes time and patience. The way to bring about change, I feel, is not through demanding it and enforcing it, but, rather, by helping people to see how the change will be for the better. The Constitution can be amended, but the Constitution is for all Americans. *All* Americans must have the right to voice what they feel is fair or unfair."

"Bah!" shouted one man sitting near the back of the room. "You're just afraid to be angry, Lincoln. Sitting around having nice chats with slave owners about why owning slaves is wrong is a laugh. I say anger and violence is the only thing they'll understand. It's the only approach that will work."

"You're entitled to your opinion, sir," Lincoln responded. "But a drop of honey catches more flies than a gallon of vinegar. Shouting at people you disagree with in order to force them to see your side rarely works."

Lincoln's new life in Springfield was busy, but he often felt out of place and even unwelcome. He was rarely invited to social events outside of the gatherings at Speed's store. Even though he was a lawyer and a legislator, many people unfairly judged him by his appearance, his accent, and his manner of speaking.

"Lincoln, though an extremely clever and well-liked fellow, is hardly up to our standards," one of the rich townspeople wrote in a note to another wealthy resident when deciding whom to invite to an annual party.

Meanwhile, in a letter to his stepmother, Lincoln wrote: "I am as lonesome here as I ever was anywhere in my life." It's true that Lincoln was not a big fan of parties and dances, but he did love meeting new people. The gatherings at Speed's store were interesting enough, but Lincoln longed for more. Thirty-two years old and single, Lincoln often thought of meeting a woman who might become his wife, though he rarely spoke of it. Finally, Lincoln began receiving invitations to parties at the home of Ninian Edwards, one of the regulars at Speed's store gatherings.

Edwards's home was richly decorated and full of expensive furniture, paintings, and tapestries. The parties were full of wealthy, important, and sometimes snobby people. Although Lincoln was a confident man, he never quite forgot his poor frontier roots. The new world of wealth and power that Lincoln often found himself surrounded by made him uneasy. He still felt rough around the edges, still a bit like that Indiana boy in ragged clothing who spoke with a Kentucky accent.

Little did Lincoln realize that it was, in fact, these rough edges that made him attractive to people—sometimes to the most unlikely people.

"Who is that?" Lincoln was standing against the back wall at one of Ninian Edwards's parties watching people dance. For some time, he had been staring at a pretty young woman who seemed to know everyone.

Joshua Speed smiled at his friend. "Why would you want to know, Abraham?" he asked teasingly.

Lincoln tugged nervously at his collar and tried to smooth out his rumpled jacket. He looked at his rough, calloused hands and then hid them behind his back.

"That's Mary Ann Todd of Lexington, Kentucky," Speed said. "She comes from quite a lot of money, and I hear that she's been educated at the finest private schools in Lexington."

"Well . . . then . . ." Lincoln began, turning away from his view of Mary.

“Oh, come on, Abraham. Go ask her to dance!” Speed said, giving his friend a little push.

“She’ll say no,” Lincoln said. “I doubt she’d be interested in someone like me.”

“But you’re wrong,” Speed said, turning Lincoln back around. “I’ve seen her look over here at you several times. Look! She just glanced over here again. You must ask her to dance!”

And so began the courtship of Lincoln and Mary Todd. Years later, Mary would recall Lincoln walking up to her that evening and saying that he wanted to dance with her “in the worst way.”

“And he certainly did!” she would joke, referring to his poor dancing.

On the surface, Lincoln and Mary could not have been less alike. Mary was barely five feet, two inches tall and rather plump. Lincoln, of course, towered above her by more than fourteen inches. Mary loved nothing more than fancy clothes and lively conversations at big parties, while Lincoln loved nothing more than reading by the fire. And Mary had been raised in a wealthy, slave-owning family, while Lincoln came from a poor family that opposed slavery.

But the two of them were a classic case of opposites attracting. Mary had grown bored with the “high-class” young men that her parents and friends insisted she go out with. She was drawn to Lincoln's honesty and awkward politeness. She had never met a man who loved poetry as much as she did—and Lincoln even *wrote* poetry. And in a time when women weren't supposed to talk about politics, Lincoln encouraged Mary to speak her mind.

As for Lincoln, he felt comfortable with Mary right away. She could talk about anything and did not seem to mind Lincoln's quiet ways. In fact, Mary's sister, Elizabeth, once wrote: "Mary always led the conversation. Lincoln would listen and gaze on her as if drawn by some power. He listened and scarcely said a word. Lincoln could not hold a long conversation with a lady—he was not educated in the female line to do so. But he was charmed by Mary's wit."

Within a year, Lincoln and Mary were engaged. But suddenly, and with no warning whatsoever, Lincoln changed his mind.

"I'm sorry, Mary. I suppose I was wrong to ever ask you to marry me." Lincoln paced the floor, his sad face sadder than ever. It had been only three weeks since he had proposed, but now he seemed determined to break the engagement.

"But why, Abraham?" Mary was in tears. "*Why?*"

"I . . ." Lincoln's voice shook and he closed his eyes. "I don't love you. That is why."

This was far from the truth. But Lincoln's fear of commitment and, perhaps, his fear of losing Mary in the same way he had lost his mother, his sister, and Ann Rutledge led him to call off the marriage.

Instantly, Lincoln was miserable. As weeks turned to months, his depression grew darker and darker. Friends began to worry that Lincoln might even take his own life. Still, Lincoln continued his work as a legislator and a lawyer through this difficult time. But things finally hit rock bottom when Joshua Speed decided to move back to Kentucky. Now, Lincoln was losing his best friend too.

"I am now the most miserable man living," he wrote to another friend during this time. "If what I feel were equally distributed to the whole human family, there would not be one cheerful face on Earth."

Finally, Lincoln had had enough. *Certainly*, he thought, *the pain of loving someone and possibly losing her could not be worse than the pain of denying the love I feel.* So, in the fall of 1842, he wrote a simple letter to Mary explaining that his feelings had never actually changed, that he had only been afraid. He apologized several times. Immediately, Mary swallowed her pride and wrote back and accepted Lincoln's apology.

And on a cold winter night just a few months later, Lincoln and Mary were married. Surrounded by only a few friends, the two exchanged their vows at the Edwardses' home, in the very same room where they had first met.

Chapter 7

"We all told you so," Elizabeth said to her sister, Mary. "Mother and Father and I all warned you about marrying someone so much beneath your class. Now look at you—living in a tavern!"

Mary Todd Lincoln held her tongue as she swept the floor in the one room she and Lincoln would know as their first "home" together. True, it was in the Globe Tavern, but it was all Lincoln could afford right now. Things would get better. Mary was certain of this.

Elizabeth walked over to the window to look down on a view of a dusty road and horses tied to a rail. Leaning on one of the horses was a filthy man drinking from a bottle of whiskey. When he was finished with the bottle, he threw it to the ground with a crash. She shook her head and sighed loudly.

"So is this what you imagined when you dreamed of married life? One room with a view of bums? And a husband who can afford no better? This would not be nearly good enough for me. I wouldn't stand for it."

Mary had had enough.

"Well, I'm *not* you!" she said angrily. "And this is good enough for me as long as I'm with Abraham. He's on his way up, and you know it. Some day . . . someday . . ." Mary paused, glaring at her sister. "Someday he's going to be president."

Elizabeth was about to laugh a scornful laugh, but she controlled herself. Smiling, she walked over and put her arm around Mary. She loved her sister; she didn't enjoy fighting with her. And she knew how terrible Mary's temper could be. It was best not to provoke her any further.

"You certainly must love him, then," Elizabeth said more gently. "That's quite a dream you have for him."

Mary folded her arms and turned away from her sister.

"It's not a dream. It's going to happen. Wait and see."

For the next few years, Lincoln worked hard at his career as a lawyer. Additionally, he was re-elected to the legislature two more times, gaining valuable political skills and becoming known as a man who stuck to his beliefs, whether or not those beliefs were the most popular. As a lawyer, he preferred to settle cases in the most peaceful and agreeable way possible. Some lawyers loved to argue loudly in the courtroom and turn every case into a dramatic fight. But this was not Lincoln's style. "As a peacemaker, the lawyer has a superior opportunity of being a good man," Lincoln often said.

During their first year living in the small room at the Globe Tavern, Mary gave birth to their first child, a son. They named him Robert after Mary's father, and from that point on, Lincoln often referred to Mary affectionately as "Mother." Lincoln had always loved children, with a sweetness and gentleness that was unusual for a young man with no children of his own. And children were always drawn to Lincoln—his height, his oversized ears, his often goofy sense of humor, and his tall top hat had made him a favorite among the children of Springfield. Now, Lincoln had a child of his own. But, of course, with the joys of fatherhood came responsibility.

"More room," Lincoln said suddenly, as he and Mary sat at their small table one evening after Robert had been rocked to sleep.

"What?" Mary asked, looking up from her sewing.

"More room," Lincoln repeated. "I believe this is what we're going to need quite soon. In fact, I wouldn't mind a bit more room at this very moment."

Mary smiled at her husband. Baby things cluttered the already cramped room. To emphasize his point, Lincoln had stuck a baby bottle in his front pocket and was delicately holding a rattle between his thumb and forefinger.

"Well, Mr. Lincoln," Mary said, using the name she often used for her husband, "what do you suggest?"

"Hmmm," Lincoln said with a mischievous look on his face. "I suggest a modest house down on the corner of Eighth and Jackson Streets."

Mary set down her sewing and stared at Lincoln. "Do you mean . . .?" she asked hopefully.

Lincoln just smiled and nodded. Finances would be tight, but Lincoln had figured out a way to afford a house of their own.

The Lincoln home on Jackson Street was small, but it was vastly bigger than anything Lincoln had ever lived in. It had a parlor, a sitting room, and a kitchen downstairs and two small bedrooms upstairs. Because the upstairs ceilings slanted, there was only a small space where Lincoln could stand upright; he spent most of his time in the upstairs rooms hunched over. Nonetheless, he and Mary loved their home. It had cost $1,200, and the Lincolns would live there for seventeen years.

These were happy years for Lincoln. His second son, Edward ("Eddie"), was born not long after the Lincolns had settled into their new home. Lincoln was a devoted and loving father, but he rarely disciplined his sons, feeling that young boys should have fun and the freedom to do as they pleased. Perhaps, because Lincoln had had a difficult childhood filled with hard work and little free time, he wanted his own sons to have an easier childhood. Perhaps he simply enjoyed watching his boys play.

During this time, Lincoln started his own law firm. His partner in the firm, Billy Herndon, was a new, young lawyer who admired Lincoln greatly. So great was Herndon's admiration for his boss, in fact, that he often grew jealous and angry about Lincoln's friendships with others. Nonetheless, the Lincoln and Herndon firm became quite successful as Lincoln's reputation for being a fair, thoughtful, and well-organized lawyer spread throughout Springfield and beyond.

The Lincoln/Herndon office on Main Street must have been a less-than-organized sight, however. Quite often, Lincoln brought his two sons to work with him and allowed them to run wild, knocking over books and scattering papers. Although Herndon generally referred to Lincoln's sons as "the brats," he endured them for the sake of the practice and his friendship with Lincoln. Some years later, Herndon described the work patterns of his soon-to-be-famous boss:

"When Lincoln reached the office, about nine o'clock in the morning, the first thing he did was to pick up a newspaper, spread himself out on an old sofa, one leg on a chair, and read aloud, much to my discomfort. Oddly enough, Lincoln never read any other way but aloud."

Other times, Herndon pointed out, Lincoln would just sprawl out on the floor and read, oblivious to the world around him. And as to Lincoln's office organization, Herndon recalled:

"Lincoln always had a bundle of papers on his desk into which he slipped anything he wished to keep and afterwards refer to. Some years ago, when removing the furniture from the office, I took down the bundle and blew from the top the coat of dust that had accumulated there. Immediately underneath the string was a slip of paper bearing this endorsement, in Lincoln's handwriting: 'When you can't find it anywhere else, look in this.'"

But what Lincoln lacked in office tact and orderliness, he made up for in striving to be the best lawyer he could be. Though Lincoln loved reading, he did not enjoy reading law manuals or textbooks about legal practice; he preferred to learn through experience and through getting to know people well. This desire to really know people was, perhaps, more important to Lincoln's law career than anything he might have learned from a law manual. Once, when a particularly difficult and rude client was driving Herndon crazy, Lincoln offered to work with him instead.

"But how can you *stand* him?" Herndon asked, shaking his head.

"At this point, I can't," Lincoln replied matter-of-factly.

"Well, then how on earth are you going to work with him?"

Lincoln thought for a while about this and finally said, "I must have a long talk with him. If I don't like a man, I must get to know him better."

By 1844, Lincoln had served as an Illinois legislator for many years. In that time, he had learned how to present his ideas strongly and clearly. He had learned how to stand up for what he believed in and how to sit quietly when it was time to listen. He had seen the best sides and the worst sides of politicians. And, most importantly, he had become filled with the desire to help make the United States an even better country than it already was. The time had come for Lincoln to move on.

"I want to run for Congress," Lincoln announced to Mary one morning.

Immediately, Mary encouraged her husband's plans. After all, a congressman helped shape laws for the entire country, not just for one state. And a congressman worked in Washington, D.C. In Mary's mind, this was one step closer to her dream of her husband becoming president of the United States—one very big step.

Lincoln did not win his first run for Congress in 1844, but he was successful the second time, in 1846. As he had done when he ran for the legislature, he spent days and weeks traveling and meeting people; only this time, he met people throughout the entire state. Not everyone agreed with Lincoln's views, but everyone certainly remembered him. Among politicians, he stood out as an unusually straightforward man. He used simple and direct language; he looked people in the eye. In the end, the majority of voters in Illinois felt Lincoln was the best man for the job.

And so in 1846, the entire Lincoln family moved to Washington, D.C. In 1846, Washington was a sprawling town of about 40,000 people. It was not a pretty town. The streets were paved with rough cobblestones that made riding in a carriage dangerous and nearly impossible. Wandering through the streets at all hours of the day and night were goats, pigs, chickens, and even cows. Many of these animals rooted through garbage and then spread it around the town. And the Capitol building was nothing like the building we see today. In 1846, the Capitol was not even half finished, and the dome was made of rough, weathered wood.

"What a filthy, ugly place!" Mary exclaimed, looking out across Pennsylvania Avenue at two chickens pecking at a moldy piece of bread. "*This* is Washington? I certainly expected something more. This doesn't even look like a place fit for women or children. What a horrid sight."

But Lincoln was not concerned with the dirty streets or half-finished Capitol. What caught his eye was significantly worse. Walking in single file, with chains attached to their feet, were a dozen or so slaves. Alongside them walked a white man with a gun and a whip.

"This can't be," Lincoln said quietly, mostly to himself. "Slaves? Here in our nation's capital? This is . . . this is surely the most horrid sight of all."

But Lincoln would find out soon enough that there were more than two thousand slaves in Washington. Worse yet, the largest slave market in the entire United States was within view of the Capitol. And so one of the first things he tried to do as a congressman was to pass a law making slavery illegal in Washington.

"I have always thought that all men should be free," Lincoln said to Congress as he argued against slavery. "But if anyone should be a slave, it should be those who support the idea of slavery! Whenever I hear a man arguing for slavery, I feel a strong desire to see it tried on him personally."

But too many congressmen opposed Lincoln's view. In 1846, there were twenty-nine states in the United States. Fifteen of the states, primarily in the North and the West, had laws against slavery, but the fourteen Southern states still allowed, and strongly supported, slavery. While Washington, D.C. was not a state, it was surrounded by states that allowed slavery. Most congressmen felt that having a small area where slavery was not allowed right in the middle of states where it *was* allowed would not be a good idea. In spite of his strong arguments, Lincoln's proposal to change the law in Washington was defeated. The slave market and ownership of other human beings would remain.

Meanwhile, Mary and the two boys were not having an easy time either. Since there were very few family homes in Washington, the Lincolns moved into a boarding house where many of the congressmen lived. Typically, congressmen did not bring their wives and children to Washington, but Lincoln had not known this. Now the entire Lincoln family was cooped up in one large room in a house full of congressmen.

Within just a few short weeks, Lincoln realized what a mistake he had made. The boys, only five and three years old, were bored and spent most of their time making noise and disturbing the other boarders. Mary, whose short temper Lincoln was becoming all too familiar with, complained bitterly about everything from the lack of good stores in Washington to the rough sheets on the bed. Soon, Mary reached the end of her very thin patience.

"I can't and won't take living here for

one more day," she announced angrily when Lincoln returned from Congress one evening. Earlier in the day, a chicken had awkwardly flapped right through the window and into the room. Mary had chased it with a broom for nearly thirty minutes before she could shoo it back out the window.

Lincoln threw his hands up in the air. "Well, what am I supposed to do? I have to stay here, Mary. Living in Washington is part of the job of a congressman."

Mary sighed and folded her arms, glaring out the window to the dirty street.

"Then *you* stay here," Mary finally said. "I'm taking the boys and going to stay with relatives in Kentucky. We can all be back together again in Springfield at the end of your term, but I'm not staying in Washington."

Not two days later, Mary and the boys were gone. Lincoln was sad to be without his family, but he understood that it was for the best for the time being. He and Mary exchanged letters faithfully during his term in Congress, and he was able to visit during holidays and time off. And without the distractions of Mary and the boys, Lincoln was able to put all his energy into Congress. He served on committees, tried to pass laws that would help the people of Illinois, and made many speeches in favor of his party, the Whigs.

Then Lincoln did something that turned many people against him.

"I would like to ask President Polk where the exact spot was that American blood was first shed," Lincoln said boldly before Congress. "Because I believe the blood was shed in Mexico—not in the United States. The United States started this war, my fellow congressmen. Our president would like us to believe that the Mexican people started this war, but I say they did not!"

Lincoln was speaking about the Mexican-American War. For some time, there had been fights about land ownership in Texas. The Mexicans still considered Texas a part of Mexico, but the United States had taken it over. And now the United States was looking to own the huge area of land that would one day become New Mexico, Arizona, Colorado, Nevada, Utah, and California. Eventually, this led to an all-out war—a war that President Polk claimed was started by the Mexican Army crossing the border and killing American soldiers. But Lincoln, and others, had evidence that this was not the way it had started at all.

Unfortunately, for Lincoln, the Mexican-American War was popular with the majority of Americans. Most people wanted to see the

United States grow larger. They didn't really care how the war had started as long as the United States won it. Some called Lincoln anti-American for trying to pinpoint who had started the war. To make matters worse, only two weeks after Lincoln had made his speech about the war, Mexico signed a treaty agreeing to give all the land in question to the United States. This made Lincoln appear foolish; it seemed as though even Mexico disagreed with him.

In the end, Lincoln's brave effort to point out the truth hurt him badly. Back in Illinois, people were embarrassed by their congressman's actions and began calling him "Spotty Lincoln" in reference to his demand to know the exact spot where the war had started. Lincoln knew that the people of Illinois would not re-elect him for a second term in Congress, so he didn't even run. Depressed and angry, Lincoln went home to Springfield to pick up where he had left off with his law practice. He wasn't sure if he would ever return to politics again.

At least I have my family, Lincoln thought as he rode a train back to Illinois. *No matter what goes wrong in this world, my wife and my boys will always be a constant bright light.*

Little did Lincoln know, as he gazed out the window at the passing fields and farm villages, just how dim that light was about to become.

Chapter 8

"I don't know, Mrs. Lincoln. I just don't know for certain." The family doctor leaned over Eddie and put a hand on the little boy's forehead. Eddie was burning up, and he seemed to be having a great deal of trouble breathing.

"But how could you not know?" Mary shouted at the doctor. "You're a doctor. Do something!"

Lincoln put his hand on Mary's shoulder, trying to calm her down. He gave the doctor a sympathetic smile and shook his head as if to indicate that his wife was overreacting.

"Mary, he's just a child. Children get sick with all sorts of little things that never amount to much," Lincoln said gently. "He'll be running around again by tomorrow morning."

But Eddie was alarmingly worse the next day, his coughing growing constant and terribly ragged. The doctor gave the Lincolns a paste made out of herbs to rub on their son's chest, but there was not much more to be done. This was a century before antibiotics and drugs would be created to fight Eddie's disease. It was, in fact, decades before doctors would even understand what Eddie Lincoln's disease was: tuberculosis.

For fifty-two days, Mary and Lincoln tended to their youngest son. But on February 1, 1850, Eddie passed away. He was buried only a few blocks from the Lincoln home. As Lincoln had done with the grave of Ann Rutledge, he often walked sadly to Eddie's grave to brush the snow aside and whisper a prayer.

Lincoln was, of course, devastated by the death of his son. Still, he forced himself to carry on and to balance his emotions for the sake of his other son, Robert. This, however, was not the case with Mary. Immediately following Eddie's death, Mary locked herself in her room for two weeks, barely coming out to eat or bathe. Lincoln would stand at her door and quietly beg her to come to the dinner table.

"Come out and eat, Mary," Lincoln said. "We must continue to live."

Lincoln's words of consolation to Mary for the next month or so were generally met with either silence or sobbing. But, as time passed, Mary's sad silence turned to anger, and then to unpredictable outbursts of rage. Sometimes, for no apparent reason at all, she would scream at Lincoln and throw books at him. Lincoln, being the calm and well-mannered person he was, tried to ignore his wife's strange temper. Once, he even caught a book in mid-air, took a look at the title, commented that he hadn't read that particular book in some time, and sat down with it.

"Lincoln and his wife got along fairly well," a neighbor once commented, "unless Mrs. Lincoln got the devil in her. Then Lincoln paid no attention—he would pick up his son and walk off."

Thankfully, Mary gave birth to a third son, William, ten months later. The new child helped to comfort both Mary and Abraham, and Mary's outbursts seemed to occur less frequently. Still, Lincoln's heart remained heavy for many years over the loss of little Eddie.

"Tell me, sir, about this fight that you say you witnessed." Lincoln was cross-examining a witness in a murder case. The trial was taking place a hundred miles away from Springfield.

"I saw James Norris," the witness said loudly, pointing to the young accused man, who was sitting next to Lincoln with a terrified expression on his face. "I saw Mr. Norris hit the man who was killed with a big club—right on the back of the head. Hard enough to kill him, I'd sure say."

Lincoln gazed at the witness, poker-faced, for several seconds.

"So you actually saw the men fighting," Lincoln clarified.

"Yes sir."

"How far away from them were you standing?"

"Far enough away that I could hide so they couldn't see me," the witness said proudly. "About 150 feet."

"I see," Lincoln said blandly. "And might I ask how you could see two men fighting from 150 feet away in the middle of the night?"

"A full moon. A very bright full moon right overhead. Practically like the sun."

"Hmmm. Yes. I see," Lincoln said absent-mindedly as he pulled a book from his messy stack of papers and notes. "Quite a puzzler, then. Quite a mystery. I wonder if you wouldn't mind reading this for the jury?"

The confused witness proceeded to read the weather reports from the night in question.

Not only had there not been a full moon; there had been heavy rain. This created such a commotion in the courtroom that the witness broke down and admitted he had lied in an attempt to cover up what had really happened. In the end, the accused murderer, eighteen-year-old Mr. Norris, was proven innocent. Norris's mother rushed up to Lincoln afterward and embraced him, weeping tears of joy. Even though Mrs. Norris had told Lincoln in advance that she had no money to pay him for his services, Lincoln had taken the case anyway.

"Mr. Lincoln! How can I ever thank you enough?" she asked between sobs.

"You just have," Lincoln said with a smile. Mrs. Norris begged Lincoln to at least come to their home for dinner, but it was time to leave. Another case waited down the road, thirty miles away.

These were Lincoln's years of being a traveling lawyer. In the 1850s, most of the brand-new small towns that were beginning to pop up in frontier areas did not have their own courts, lawyers, or judges. And most of the people, when they had legal problems, could not afford the time and expense of traveling one hundred miles or more to go to a court. As a result, the court came to them.

Lincoln traveled with several other lawyers and a judge. All in all, the group covered more than five hundred miles, all of it on horseback, since trying to get carriages through muddy back roads often took twice as long. The traveling lawyers and judge were gone for three months in the spring and three months in the fall. And while Lincoln missed his family, he loved the life of a touring lawyer.

When the court came to some of these small towns, it was the most entertainment many of the residents would see all year. Frontier villages had no theaters, so the "performances" of the lawyers were attended by nearly everyone. Townspeople would cram into the general store, barn, or storage building that was being used as a makeshift courtroom. Some people even brought picnics. Without a doubt, a roomful of people offering their undivided attention brought out the best in Lincoln.

"Let me tell you all a sad but true little tale," Lincoln said to a large group in Beardstown, Illinois. Lincoln often told stories before the legal proceedings began, well aware that the crowds had come to be entertained. He was so well liked that, in time, he became something of a star on that particular Illinois circuit.

"Just the other day," Lincoln began, "as we were all riding on horseback to the next town, a lovely young lady approached us, also on horseback. As she grew nearer, I stopped to let her pass. She also stopped and stared at me closely with an odd expression on her face.

"'I do believe you're the ugliest man I ever saw,' she finally said.

"'Madam, you are probably right, but I can't help it,' I replied.

"'No, you can't help it,' the woman answered. 'But you could have stayed home.'"

Lincoln, being the excellent comedian that he was, never cracked a smile as the townspeople burst into laughter.

Even as he moved through questioning in the temporary courtrooms, Lincoln often amused people with his unusual approaches. During one case, it was embarrassingly clear that the person on trial was lying. Although it had been proven that the accused had been present at the crime scene, he continued to deny it. In the accused man's mind, if he simply disagreed with the facts, then the facts would be changed.

"So, you say you were not there even though we have proof that you were?" Lincoln asked in his calm drawl.

"I was *not* there," the defendant said stubbornly, folding his arms. "And if I say I wasn't, I wasn't."

"Well, let me ask you this," Lincoln continued. "How many legs does a dog have if you call his tail a leg?"

The courtroom filled with snickers as the defendant looked confused.

"I reckon five, if you say the tail's a leg."

"No sir," Lincoln concluded. "Four. *Saying* that a tail is a leg doesn't make it a leg."

Clearly, the people of southern Illinois could hardly wait until Lincoln returned to town six months later for another "show."

"I know there is a God and that He hates injustice and slavery. I see the storm coming, and I know that His hand is in it. If He has a place for me, and I think He has, I believe I am ready."

Lincoln spoke these words five years after leaving Washington. When he left, he had been disappointed with politics and politicians; he had felt that maybe he didn't really have a place in the political world and that perhaps he'd be better off as a lawyer. So, for five years, Lincoln had lived the pleasant and often entertaining life of a traveling lawyer. But in his heart, he missed being in the middle of all the controversies, the decisions, the battles, and the successes that took place in Washington.

Then, in 1854, something happened that made Lincoln so angry that he could no longer sit quietly in Springfield.

Years earlier, in 1820, when there had been only twenty-two states in the United States, eleven had allowed slavery, and eleven had laws against it. When Missouri and Maine were added as states, Congress decided to keep the balance of slave and free states by allowing Missouri to have slaves while Maine would remain a free state. This was known as the "Missouri Compromise." But the most important part of this compromise was that it was also agreed that all remaining land north of Missouri's southern border would forever have laws against slavery.

Thirty-four years later, a senator from Illinois, Stephen Douglas, decided to present a bill to Congress that would totally change the Missouri Compromise. Douglass thought it would be a better idea if the people who lived in Kansas and Nebraska—both of which were free states according to the Compromise—could just decide for themselves whether or not slavery should be allowed. This bill became known as the "Kansas-Nebraska Act."

Lincoln, along with all people who opposed slavery, was horrified and furious. He and Douglas had long opposed each other on both political and personal issues—Douglas was a Democrat, and he had once dated and hoped to marry Mary—but their disagreements had never spurred Lincoln to action. This one, however, did.

Lincoln no longer held a political office, but the people of Illinois knew him well. When word spread that Abraham Lincoln was going to give a speech at the Illinois State Fair against slavery and the Kansas-Nebraska Act, thousands of people jammed the fairgrounds to hear him.

"I hate this act because of the monstrous injustice of slavery itself," Lincoln shouted out to the crowd that October afternoon. "I am not here today to speak of *abolishing* slavery. After all, it is allowed by the Constitution. But the Founding Fathers hid it away as an afflicted man hides away a cancer which he dares not cut out all at once for fear of bleeding to death. However, we must not allow slavery to continue to spread!"

As always, Lincoln wanted to be fair. Although he hated slavery, he understood that, by law, it must be allowed to continue in the original states where slavery had been protected by the Constitution. But Lincoln feared that, like a cancer, the growth of slavery would eventually destroy the United States.

The Southern states felt just the opposite. Many of the people in these states felt that *not* allowing slavery in new states would eventually lead to a Constitutional amendment outlawing slavery in their own states. This, they felt, would be the ruin of the South—and they would not stand for it. Rather quickly, the entire country was becoming strongly divided on the issue of slavery. This, then, was the "storm" that Lincoln had seen coming. Already, vicious fights over slavery were breaking out in Kansas, and some of the Southern states began murmuring about splitting from the United States completely (an act called "seceding" or "secession") and forming their own separate country. Lincoln knew that his days of staying out of politics had come to an end. It was time to take action.

"A house divided against itself cannot stand. I believe this government cannot endure, permanently half slave and half free . . . I do not expect the house to fall—but I do expect it will cease to be divided. It will become all one thing or all the other."

Lincoln stood before the crowd at the 1858 Illinois Republican Convention and spoke boldly against slavery. Lincoln's party, the Whigs, had re-formed as a new party, the Republicans, whose main message was that the spread of slavery was wrong. And now Lincoln was running against Stephen Douglas to become the United States senator from Illinois.

For most of the year, Douglas and Lincoln had traveled throughout Illinois, debating each other in numerous towns and cities. Their styles, in more ways than one, were completely different. Douglas was quite short, loved fancy clothes, and insisted on traveling in luxury. Lincoln, of course, was just as happy in an old coat, traveling around on horseback. In debate, Douglas was fiery and angry. Lincoln was thoughtful and calm.

"If you want Negro citizenship," Douglas barked out at one debate after another, "if you want to allow them into Illinois to settle with the white man, if you want them to have the same rights as the white man, then support Mr. Lincoln and his Republican party. I warn you now—Mr. Lincoln will even allow Negroes and whites to marry!"

This statement never failed to shock and upset a crowd. In 1858, most of those who were against slavery still did not believe that black people were the same as white people. They felt that blacks, although human, were inferior. They did not think that human beings should be slaves, but they also felt that blacks were a different kind of human and should not be given all of the same freedoms and rights as whites. In courts of law during this time, black people were often denied their rights because judges felt they were inferior human beings.

Lincoln argued back that he was *not* in favor of blacks marrying whites or even allowing blacks to vote—yet. It is tempting to imagine that Lincoln supported total equality for black people, but that would be a very long time coming. Lincoln wanted to stop slavery, but his views of black people in comparison to white people were not much different from many white people's views in 1858:

"I am not in favor of bringing about the social and political equality of the white and black races," Lincoln explained at one debate. "There must be the position of superior and inferior, and I, as much as any other man, am in favor of having the superior position assigned to the white race."

Still, Lincoln stood firmly opposed to enslaving black people. "We will not have peace in this country until the opponents of slavery stop the spread of it," Lincoln said. "The slave is my equal and the equal of Mr. Douglas. The slave is human and the equal of every living man!"

Lincoln debated Douglas until he was hoarse and exhausted. He was cheered loudly from town to town, but in the end, Douglas's fear tactics worked: Lincoln lost his race for the Senate.

"I feel like the boy who stumped his toe," Lincoln said with a sad smile to a group of friends after his loss. "I am too big to cry and too badly hurt to laugh."

True, the Senate seat would not be Lincoln's. But bigger things were in store. Indeed, God would have a place for Lincoln.

Chapter 9

"I, John Brown, am now quite certain that the crimes of this guilty land can only be washed away with blood! I will go to my death now and mingle my blood with the blood of millions in this slave country."

These were the final words of the fierce and violent abolitionist, John Brown, before he was led to the gallows and hanged. Brown had attempted to put together an army of both white men and slaves. He had hoped that this army would make successful attacks on slave owners and then become bigger and stronger as the slaves of killed owners would join the ranks and fight. His plan was to start near Virginia and move steadily south. Brown truly believed that, in the end, slavery would be destroyed, and slave owners would be left either dead or powerless.

One of Brown's first stops on his march south was a gun and ammunitions armory in Harper's Ferry, Virginia. Brown wanted to take over the armory and use the weapons to arm his soldiers. It seemed a simple enough plan, but word got out to the neighboring towns, and soon Brown and his men were surrounded. Panicking, Brown's group killed a number of innocent people before being captured and, eventually, sent to their deaths by hanging.

Immediately, this bloody event sent shock waves throughout the United States. Many abolitionists in the northern states saw Brown as something of a hero and pointed to his hanging as proof that the U.S. government supported slavery. Meanwhile, many in the southern states used Brown as an example of how dangerous and irrational the abolitionists could be. The murmurs of seceding were now becoming angrier and angrier shouts.

Back in Springfield, Lincoln read the news and sighed sadly. *Surely*, he thought, rubbing his head, *there must be a way to resolve this issue peacefully. And, no matter what, we cannot allow this country to split into two separate countries over this issue. The United States must not fail.*

As Lincoln sat at the kitchen table, a worried look on his face, a young boy came running as fast as he could and jumped up into Lincoln's lap.

"Don't frown, Daddy. It makes funny lines on your face!" he said with a giggle, pointing to Lincoln's forehead. A broad grin replaced Lincoln's frown.

"All right then, Tad," Lincoln said as he picked up the boy and put him on his shoulders. "Enough news for today. Let's take a walk into town."

Thomas "Tad" Lincoln had been born in 1853. Lincoln nicknamed him Tad because he felt his son's head was too big for his body—like a tadpole's head. Tad would be the last son born to Mary and Lincoln, and, because he was the baby of the family, Lincoln spoiled him even more than he had spoiled his other sons. The two were often inseparable, Lincoln carrying his son on his shoulders downtown, to the office, and up and down the stairs of their home.

But even the pleasant distraction of his youngest son was not enough to keep the worry lines off Lincoln's face. Although Lincoln had lost his Senate campaign, he vowed to himself that he would not sit still and watch slavery continue to spread throughout the land he loved so dearly. If he could not make a difference in the Senate, he would do it elsewhere.

On May 29, 1856, the newly formed Republican Party of Illinois met officially for the first time in Bloomington, Illinois. Lincoln was scheduled to be a speaker, so, as usual, huge crowds gathered. The country was reaching a boiling point over the issue of slavery, and no one was more passionate about ending slavery than Abraham Lincoln. Everyone expected a powerful speech. But no one was prepared for just how incredible it would be.

"I have heard or read all of Mr. Lincoln's great speeches," said Billy Herndon, Lincoln's law partner. "And it is my opinion that the Bloomington speech was the greatest effort of his life. If Lincoln was six feet four inches high usually, at Bloomington that day he was seven feet, and inspired at that."

The audience members were so stunned that they sat motionless and barely breathing as Lincoln spoke. The newspaper reporters were so stunned that they forgot to write anything in their reporters' journals. Not one person in that hall that day ever forgot Lincoln's speech, but no one made a written record of it, either. Thus, it became famously known as "The Forgotten Speech."

It was, perhaps, the effect that this speech had on its audience that began to propel Lincoln to national fame over the next few years. Slowly, an undercurrent of chatter grew about nominating Lincoln as the Republican candidate for president of the United States in the 1860 race. Lincoln laughed at the idea of becoming president when, after all, he hadn't even been able to win a Senate seat. But Mary was thrilled.

"Mr. Lincoln," she said in great seriousness, "you had better begin to stand up straighter and pay more attention to how you dress. For heaven's sake, the next president cannot go around wearing one brown sock and one black sock!"

Lincoln smiled at his wife and nodded, but he still forgot to button the middle button on his shirt. He still didn't care about the dust on his top hat or the wrinkles in his coat. And when reporters began to follow Lincoln around town, asking what he thought of his chances of being the next president, Lincoln laughed out loud and replied, "Just think of such a sucker as me as president. I must, in honesty, say I do not think myself fit for the presidency."

Still, Lincoln's fame grew in spite of himself. And with it, his confidence in the idea of being president grew. As the 1860 Republican Convention loomed, Lincoln sat down one evening to write a letter to his oldest son, Robert, who was now away at school in New Hampshire. Alone with his thoughts by the fireside, Lincoln was able to admit to himself that he *had* been thinking about the presidency. And so his oldest son was the first to read about it in his father's own handwriting: *When not a very great man begins to be mentioned for a very great position, his head is likely to be turned. So I will be entirely frank. The taste is in my mouth a little.* Yes, Lincoln was confident enough to consider running for president, but in his typical humorous and modest fashion, he also added: *This, no doubt, disqualifies me, to some extent, to form correct opinions.*

"Call the roll! Call the roll!"

It was May 16, 1860, and the Republican National Convention in Chicago was nominating a candidate for president. Thousands of men gathered to see how the voting would go. State by state, delegates cast their votes; and as they did, the new tally, or "roll," was announced. The top two candidates were William Seward of New York and Abraham Lincoln of Illinois. Everyone had been certain that Seward, a very famous and powerful man, would win the nomination. But slowly, Lincoln was gaining votes. And as is typical, most of those gathered wanted to see an underdog win. Since the convention was being held in the state of Illinois, seeing Illinois' "favorite son" gaining ground was particularly exciting.

"Call the roll! Call the roll!"

The chairman, a short man with heavy glasses, moved to the center of the stage and shouted out, "Seward, 174 votes. Lincoln, 102."

Time passed, and more votes were cast. Lincoln continued to inch closer to Seward.

"Seward, 185. Lincoln, 181," the chairman bellowed as the voting neared the end.

The entire crowd went crazy. A total of 233 votes was needed to win the nomination. It now appeared that Lincoln might really become the nominee. When the third roll was called, Lincoln had pulled ahead of Seward and needed only three and a half more votes. An anxious buzz filled the hall as all in attendance awaited the final outcome.

Suddenly, a delegate from Ohio jumped up.

"I rise, Mr. Chairman," the young man said in a very nervous voice, "to announce the change of four of our votes to Mr. Lincoln."

The hall burst into pandemonium. A cannon on the roof of the building was fired to signal the victory of Illinois' own candidate.

Meanwhile, Lincoln and his supporters waited back home in Springfield for the news. Lincoln was so certain that he wouldn't win that he had gone with a friend to play handball at an outside court. But around the time that the telegram was to come in, Lincoln returned to the office of the local newspaper, the *Illinois State Journal.* When the telegram arrived, Lincoln read it aloud: *We did it. Glory to God.*

Friends and supporters cheered and danced and passed the telegram around the office. Lincoln just smiled and shook hands. Occasionally, he also shook his head in disbelief. It was still a wonder to him that he, a poor boy from Kentucky with no formal education or real experience with national government, had just received his party's nomination for president of the United States. Finally he held out his hand for the telegram.

"Well, gentlemen," Lincoln said with a sheepish grin, "there is a little short woman at our house who is probably more interested in this telegram than I am; and if you will excuse me, I will take it up and let her see it."

When election time came in November 1860, Lincoln's chances looked quite good. Lincoln had campaigned tirelessly throughout the West and the North. Because Southerners did not support Lincoln, he steered clear of most Southern states. The northern and western supporters of Lincoln used split logs, or rails, as a symbol, since his hard labor in his younger years as a rail-splitter struck people as honest, real work—the kind of work they'd want him to do as president. In town after town, parades featured floats covered with split rails. Stages where Lincoln gave speeches were piled with rails.

And, like Lincoln's trademark rails, the Democratic Party was now split in half. It had chosen two candidates instead of one, and this was not good news for the Democrats. Since the man with the greatest number of votes would win, it seemed that, since his entire party supported Lincoln, there was no way Lincoln could lose.

And he didn't.

The election was not a landslide, but Lincoln won by a decent majority of votes. Amazingly, *not one vote* from the South had been cast for Lincoln. Southerners, fearing Lincoln would ultimately end slavery everywhere, stood strongly and entirely against him. And when Lincoln won, many in the South looked to the future with gloom and doom.

"The evil days are now upon us!" wrote the *Dallas Herald*.

"The South must arm itself at once," reported the *Augusta Constitutionalist*.

The talk in the South about seceding from the rest of the United States in order to save itself was now a very real discussion. But Republicans did not, at first, take the South seriously. Even Lincoln assumed that Southerners were merely irritated by his winning the election and that things would calm down soon enough.

"The people of the South have too much good sense and good temper to attempt the ruin of the government," Lincoln said not long after winning. His main message during his run for the presidency had been that slavery could not spread and continue to "divide" the country. Little did Lincoln know just how divided the United States was about to become.

For a short time after the election, Lincoln relaxed and celebrated with those Americans who were thrilled with his win. He attended many parties and personally thanked thousands of supporters. He even did a favor for an eleven-year-old fan. Right before being elected, Lincoln had received the following letter:

Dear Sir,

I am a little girl only 11 years old, but want you to be president of the United States very much so I hope you won't think me very bold to write to such a great man as you are. Have you any little girls about as large as I am? I have got 4 brothers and they will vote for you if you

let your whiskers grow. You would look a great deal better, because your face is so thin. All the ladies like whiskers and they would tease their husbands to vote for you and then you would be president.

Grace Bedell

Although we picture Abraham Lincoln as the tall man with the dark beard and sideburns, it had never occurred to him to grow a beard until he received this letter from little Grace Bedell. Not one to spend much time fiddling with his own appearance, Lincoln questioned Grace's request:

My dear little Miss,

I regret the necessity of saying I have no daughters—I have three sons—one seventeen, one nine, and one seven years of age—They, with their mother, constitute my whole family—As to the whiskers, having never worn any, do you not think people would call it a piece of silly affectation if I were to begin it now?

Your very sincere well-wisher,
A. Lincoln

Nonetheless, after winning the election, Lincoln granted his young fan's wish and grew his trademark beard. Mary Lincoln did not care at all for her husband's new look, but she had more important things to think about. Her prediction from years earlier had come true: Lincoln would be inaugurated the sixteenth president of the United States in fewer than four months! Mary, clearly the exact opposite of her husband, went on a clothes-buying spree of immense proportions. She purchased nearly a dozen ball gowns, as well as the finest silk gloves and most beautiful jewelry to complement them.

Lincoln was, perhaps, as bothered by Mary's spending as she had been by his beard. But he too had more important things to concern him. As the March inauguration day grew nearer, death threats became a common occurrence. As Lincoln traveled up to Washington by train, stopping in towns along the way to speak, threatening notes were often pushed under his hotel room doors. And when the train finally neared Washington, he was quietly switched to a secret train in the middle of the night. Lincoln's aides had received a letter from assassins who claimed they would be waiting along the tracks in Baltimore.

All of these would-be assassins were angry Southerners (and, occasionally, pro-slavery Northerners) who wanted Lincoln gone before he could even be sworn in. But Lincoln was not overly concerned with these threats.

"Why would anyone in his right mind actually send a letter outlining how he was going to kill me?" Lincoln asked with a laugh. "If a man were intent on doing away with me, I assume he'd do so without the courtesy of letting me know about it in advance."

Lincoln even kept a file of particularly ridiculous or amusing death threats. Still, he was not foolish—he always took the advice and warning of his aides very seriously. He was well aware that there were many people in the United States who were terribly upset with his winning the presidency.

Then, on December 20, 1860, Lincoln became even more aware of how upset the South really was.

"We, the people of the State of South Carolina in convention assembled, do declare that the Union now subsisting between South Carolina and other States, under the name of 'the United States of America,' is hereby dissolved."

This was the announcement that rocked the entire nation. South Carolina became the first state to secede from the United States, or the "Union," as it was called. Then, like dominoes, other Southern states fell into line.

Before Lincoln was even inaugurated, Florida, Mississippi, Alabama, Georgia, Louisiana, and Texas had all seceded from the Union. These states even elected their *own* president, Jefferson Davis, and called themselves the "Confederate States of America."

Lincoln was terribly sad about this turn of events. As passionate as he was about ending slavery, Lincoln was equally passionate about not letting the United States break into two separate countries. More than once, he stated that the idea "broke his heart."

On the morning of March 4, 1861, Lincoln stood in a cold winter wind on the steps of the nation's capitol, his tall hat in his hand. He had struggled over his inaugural address to the country. Many of his advisors had told him to be firm, even threatening, with the Southern states.

"This is illegal, Mr. Lincoln! States cannot just decide to leave the country if they're unhappy with something," one advisor said in disgust.

"Let these troublemakers know that you have the power to imprison every one of them," another advised. "Remind them that the U.S. Army can put them in their place rather quickly."

But Lincoln did not wish to choose an angry path. More than anything, he wished to avoid a war between the states. In his heart, he believed common ground could and must be found.

"We are not enemies, but friends," Lincoln said emotionally that morning. He paused to look around. Sharpshooters stood along the rooftops, watching for trouble. Police and soldiers lined the streets, watching the crowds closely. Lincoln frowned and continued.

"We must not be enemies! Though passion may have strained, it must not break our bonds of affection. The chords of memory, stretching from every battlefield and grave, to every living heart all over this land, will yet swell the chorus of the Union when touched by the better angels of our nature."

Lincoln felt that all people, regardless of their politics, had "better angels" within them. He believed that the pride and love American citizens had for their country would surely defeat a hatred that could break it apart. And, so, Abraham Lincoln called on these "better angels" of human nature to put an end to the bitterness that threatened to destroy the United States.

But it was too late. The angels had disappeared, and the storm had arrived.

Chapter 10

"Mr. President, sir, the Confederacy has taken over Fort Sumter in Charleston, South Carolina!" William Seward, the Secretary of State, rushed into Lincoln's office. Seward's face was white, and his hands shook.

Lincoln looked up from his work, confusion in his eyes. He had been in office for only two weeks. "Taken over? But that is a federal fort guarded by federal troops. How can they have taken it over?"

"The fort has been surrounded, sir," Seward explained. "They won't let Major Anderson or any of his soldiers out of the fort. And they won't allow any food or water to be brought in."

Lincoln sat silently for a minute or more, his forehead wrinkled in thought and worry.

Other forts throughout the South had already been taken over by the "Confederacy," the new name given to the group of Southern states that had separated from the United States. The forts had been taken over rather easily while President Buchanan had still been in office. Buchanan had not wanted to become involved in the troubles between the North and the South; he preferred to leave the mess for the next president.

Now the Confederacy wanted to test Lincoln. They knew that Lincoln clearly opposed the taking over of federal forts; after all, it was against the law. But now the states in the Confederacy saw themselves as their own country. They didn't have to follow the laws of the United States, much less the wishes of a president they hadn't elected.

"How much food and supplies do Major Anderson and his troops have?" Lincoln finally asked quietly.

Seward stared at Lincoln in disbelief and shook his head. "Sir, surely you aren't thinking of waiting it out and seeing what happens. We must send troops down to Charleston immediately. We cannot allow the Confederacy to get the upper hand."

"No. No troops," Lincoln said firmly. "If we send troops, a war will begin, and the North will be blamed for starting it. I want to avoid a war at all costs. Certainly you can see that a war between the states, a civil war, will damage our country—perhaps beyond repair."

Seward nodded. He didn't completely agree with Lincoln, but he understood. "Well, I would estimate that there are enough supplies for maybe two weeks or a little less."

Time passed, and the Confederacy did not leave its positions surrounding the fort. Lincoln grew deeply discouraged. Word came to him that supplies at Fort Sumter were nearly gone. The men trapped inside would soon begin starving. Lincoln must take some sort of action.

Mr. Governor, Lincoln wrote to the governor of South Carolina, *we are sending supplies to Major Anderson and his men. If such attempts are not resisted, no effort to send troops, arms, or ammunition will be made.*

Lincoln explained that he did not want conflict; he simply wanted to help the men inside Fort Sumter. But the governor viewed the approaching supply ships as a threat. Immediately, word was sent to Major Anderson that he must surrender the fort, or else shots would be fired upon Fort Sumter within the hour. Anderson refused to surrender. So, at 4:30 on the morning of April 12, 1861, the Confederate troops that had surrounded Fort Sumter for two weeks finally raised their rifles and let the bullets fly. The Civil War had begun.

"I couldn't get down here to the courthouse fast enough to sign up!"

"Just give me my rifle and my orders, and I'm ready to fight for my country."

"The other side will never know what hit them once they see *our* troops coming up over the hillsides. They'll go crying for their mothers!"

"They're gonna wish they never started this war."

In both the North and the South, the conversations among young men rushing to volunteer for service were almost identical. Each side blamed the other for starting the war. Each side had supreme confidence that *it* would win the war. Lincoln had put out the call for 75,000 volunteers for the Union militia. In the Confederacy, Jefferson Davis called for even more soldiers.

To many of these young soldiers, the issue of slavery had very little to do with why they were eager to fight. The Northern soldiers fought to keep the United States whole. They knew, like Lincoln, that if the country were to split in half, both halves would be considerably weaker than the United States had been. And it would be likely that both the Confederacy and the Union would forever be bitter toward one another.

Southern soldiers fought for the right of individual states to make decisions for themselves. Southerners had long felt that the North, in general, and the U.S. government, in particular, interfered too much in their lives. The issue of slavery had simply brought these feelings to a boiling point. However, 90 percent or more of the soldiers came from families who had never even owned slaves. Many Southerners even opposed slavery, but this did not keep them from fighting in the Civil War. The sense of pride and the desire to defend their home was too strong.

And as lines were drawn, more Southern states joined the Confederacy: Virginia, Arkansas, North Carolina, and Tennessee. The border states of Kentucky, Missouri, and Maryland were states that allowed slavery but did not end up joining the Confederacy. Because of this, relatives who might live only five miles apart (near the Kentucky/Tennessee border, for example) could end up being in states that opposed one another in the war. Brothers would ultimately face one another on the battlefields.

"But this will be a short war," one Southern mayor proclaimed at a town gathering. "I promise to use my handkerchief to wipe up all the blood that will be spilled."

The crowd laughed, but it was uneasy laughter. The North was bigger, and it had more people, more supplies, and more power.

"What makes you think this here war's gonna be so short?" a man standing up front shouted.

The mayor grinned and shook his finger for emphasis. "Because they don't expect us to really fight. They think we'll back down as soon as the first real battle gets going. As soon as they see we're serious, they'll leave us be."

Up in Washington, Lincoln, too, believed the war would be brief. But it was not because he didn't think the Confederacy was serious; Lincoln simply believed that the North was so much more powerful and well prepared for battle than the South that, after one quick battle, the South would surrender. Lincoln remained fairly calm and confident about the entire situation—until a rainy week in April, just a week after the call for volunteer soldiers.

Where are they? Why don't they come? Lincoln said nervously to himself as he paced the floor in the Executive Office of the Capitol. From the window, he could see the Potomac River. For days, the city of Washington had been waiting for the ships full of Union soldiers to arrive from the north. Bordering Washington to the south was Virginia, a Confederate state, and the Confederates were making the best of Washington's unprotected situation.

Bit by bit, the Confederate troops had cut Washington off from the rest of the United States. Mail was not allowed through, ships were blocked from entering Chesapeake Bay, telegraph lines were cut, and even railroad lines and bridges were torn up. So many residents of Washington had fled north that the city looked like a ghost town. For nearly a week, Lincoln privately worried, paced, and became truly afraid that the Confederacy would take over and destroy the nation's capital. In desperation, he called for troops from Maryland to protect Washington. Bringing troops from Maryland was risky since even though it was not a Confederate state, many of the people who lived there sided with the Confederacy.

"But Mr. President," a reporter shouted to him when word got out that soldiers were being called from this border state, "there are more than 75,000 residents of Maryland who support the South, not the North. And they say they will oppose these troops."

"Well, then," Lincoln replied dryly, "I presume they have room in Maryland for 75,000 graves."

Lincoln may have had a tough exterior, but inside he was shaking. No one was more relieved than he when ships packed with Union soldiers finally steamed down the Potomac.

While Abraham Lincoln was facing some of the most difficult times of his political life, Mary Lincoln was having more fun than she had ever had before. If she had been worried about returning to Washington, D.C., with its filthy streets and unfinished buildings, all worries disappeared upon arriving.

"Twenty thousand dollars!" Mary exclaimed when Lincoln explained to her how much money Congress was allotting for fixing up and decorating the White House. (Twenty thousand dollars was equal to nearly a quarter of a million dollars in today's money.)

"Yes, but try not to spend it all in one afternoon, dear," Lincoln said with a deadpan expression.

"Mr. Lincoln, you need not worry." Mary said, "I have, as you well know, excellent budgeting skills."

Lincoln looked up from his newspaper with mock confusion. "How long have I known this? And you say I know it well?"

Mary rolled her eyes at her husband.

"In all seriousness, though," Lincoln said, "this money is allotted for the *entire* four years of our stay here in the White House. Once it's gone, it's gone. So spend it wisely, and"—here, Lincoln leaned forward for emphasis—"make it last, Mary. Four years."

"Of course, Mr. Lincoln."

This was April 1861. By October, barely six months later, every penny of the twenty thousand dollars was gone. Mary had traveled to Philadelphia and New York City to buy the finest carpeting, silk drapes, and furniture. Satin wallpaper had been imported from France, and gold inlaid china had been shipped from Belgium. Without a doubt, Mary Lincoln transformed the White House from the dingy and poorly decorated building it had been to the elegant home we know it as today. Never had there been such a First Lady in the White House; Mary Lincoln certainly left her mark.

However, Mary's mark came with a price—and it was more than twenty thousand dollars. When Mary had begun running out of money, she became angry and desperate. She flew into a rage at anyone who questioned her spending. Decorators and aides began referring to her as "the Hell-cat." And Lincoln, with the nation's fate in his hands, certainly had more important things to do than worry about his wife's spending patterns. Never one to have paid much attention to fancy clothes or elegant furnishings, Lincoln had no idea what his wife had done.

"I'll tell you what to do," the White House gardener, John Watt, said in a low voice to Mary one afternoon. She had confided in John about spending all the money. She *had* to tell someone, and she figured the gardener would keep a secret. Eventually, she even asked for his advice.

"Just pad the bills," John said casually. "And make up bills for things you don't even buy. It's done all the time around here. It'll be fine."

Mary, of course, knew this was wrong, but she didn't want to stop spending. It had become an addiction. This went on for some time until, as it always does when one "spends" money he or she doesn't have, Mary found herself in a serious hole. Wringing her hands, she went to Lincoln and explained what she had done.

"You *WHAT*?" It was one of the few times Mary saw her husband lose his temper.

"But can't you ask Congress for additional funding?" Mary asked persistently. "After all, it's for the White House; it's for the *president*!"

If steam could have blown out of Lincoln's big ears, it would have at that point.

"Never!" he shouted, "Never will I ask Congress for more funding for flub dubs for this damned old house! Can you imagine the stink it would make if the country found out that twenty thousand dollars for furnishing the White House had been overspent by the president when poor, freezing soldiers don't even have blankets?"

Mary couldn't argue with this, but she still could not be convinced that Congress wouldn't hand over more funding. In the end, Congress somehow learned, through a third party, of Mary's careless spending, and it quietly increased the amount of money that could be spent on the White House.

Lincoln was angry and embarrassed. In apologizing to Congress, he simply said, "My friends, this is sad evidence that when we feel prosperity, we often forget what is right."

Three months after the takeover of Fort Sumter by the Confederates, the first real battle of the Civil War was about to take place. The Confederate uniforms were grey, while the Union uniforms were blue. The North was so confident that the boys in blue would win this battle that cartoons were drawn of giant blue tidal waves crashing down on tiny grey soldiers.

The battle plan was simple enough. Lincoln had given his top general, General Irvin McDowell, orders to attack the Confederate troops on July 9, 1861 in Manassas, Virginia (not far from Washington), in a wide grassy area known as Bull Run. McDowell knew his troops were inexperienced, but he wasn't particularly worried. He was certain that the "rebels," as the Confederate troops were called, would turn and run as soon as they saw the Union troops with their better rifles, their brighter uniforms, and their greater numbers. McDowell even decided to delay the battle by nearly a week as he fiddled around with sneak attack plans and fancy strategies.

On the morning of July 21, thousands of Union soldiers marched toward Bull Run. Behind them trailed dozens of Washingtonians with their picnic baskets. Everyone, from families with children to congressmen, assumed that this "battle" would be like a sporting event. They thought it would be lovely to sit up on the hillside and watch the boys in grey run away from the boys in blue. Then they would toast their champions, give them a loud cheer, and follow them back to Washington.

But things didn't quite work out that way.

"Hold your fire until they come within fifty yards!" shouted General "Stonewall" Jackson to his Confederate troops. "Then fire your bullets at them and stab them with your bayonets. And when you run toward them, shout at the top of your lungs like Furies!"

Meanwhile, General McDowell was taken by surprise. Because the battle had been delayed by a week, the Confederate troops were already in place at Bull Run—*they* were the ones with the sneak attack.

As 30,000 Confederate troops came screaming toward the Union soldiers—a tactic that would become known as the "rebel yell"—McDowell panicked. "Retreat! Retreat!" he screamed frantically to his troops. The troops turned and ran for their lives back up a hill not far from the picnickers. Gunshots and howls followed close on the heels of the Union soldiers. Terrified, the picnickers fled back down the other side of the hill, leaving their blankets and baskets behind. Legend has it that one famous congressman was so frightened that he ran all the way back to Washington with a napkin tucked into his shirt. It was a story that amused people for many years.

But back in Washington, Lincoln was not amused at all. The top general Lincoln had chosen had failed miserably, so Lincoln blamed himself for the Union's loss at Bull Run. Rather than waste time listening to McDowell's excuses, Lincoln fired him. Then, immediately, Lincoln assigned a new top general, George McClellan, to try his hand with the troops.

When the dust settled and the hot, red sun rose the next morning, Lincoln went to Bull Run to survey the damage. Nearly 800 corpses were scattered across the grassy field. Hundreds more soldiers, all of them about the age of Lincoln's oldest son, lay wounded and crying out for help. Lincoln put his head in his hands. This would be neither a quick nor an easy war.

"If Hell is not any more than this," Lincoln said through gritted teeth, "then Hell holds no terror for me."

Chapter 11

My dear General McClellan,
If you don't want to use the army,
I should like to borrow it for a while.
Yours respectfully,
Abraham Lincoln

After the next few battles, Lincoln sent this short note to his new general as something of a joke, but he was also honestly frustrated with McClellan. The top general was excellent at training the Union troops and teaching them all the details of how to be the best soldiers. However, McClellan was reluctant to actually ever *fight*. He often waited too long to make a move, and when he finally took action, it was too late. As a result, the Union continued to lose battles.

Lincoln received one discouraging report after another during the long, bloody year of 1862. In battles throughout the Shenandoah Valley and in Fredericksburg, the number of soldiers killed, on both sides, was overwhelming. In the Battle of Shiloh, more than 24,000 men were killed—more than all the Americans killed in the entire Revolutionary War!

It is important to remember that the population of the United States in 1862 was only one tenth of what it is today. So when Lincoln received news that 24,000 Americans had died in one battle alone, it was like being told that nearly a quarter of a million Americans had died. To a man like Lincoln, whose heart went out even to an injured dog, the war was unbearable.

Civil War battlegrounds were horribly gruesome. Most of the battles involved tens of thousands of men literally rushing toward one another, their guns, swords, and bayonets at the ready. In this type of hand-to-hand fighting, there were usually more injuries than deaths. The injured were brought to Civil War field hospitals—often little more than filthy tents with crude operating tools. Anesthesia was not common; during painful operations, soldiers were simply given whiskey and told to bite down on a bullet. These were the conditions under which limbs were sawed off, bullets dug out, and skulls taped back together—by the thousands.

But as deeply as the Civil War pained Lincoln, he was determined that the South would not win.

"I sincerely hope it does not come to this," Lincoln said to his Cabinet in 1863, "but I will make the South a graveyard before I will see slavery triumph or see a successful secession destroy the United States."

And so Lincoln tried out new generals. But each new one was either too afraid or too inexperienced to fight battles well. Meanwhile, the South had two very strong generals: Robert E. Lee and "Stonewall" Jackson. Lincoln had originally asked Lee to lead the Union army, but Lee had said no. Even though Lee opposed slavery, he was from Virginia and would not fight against his beloved South. He, like so many other soldiers, would not turn against family.

Lee was excellent with strategy and attack plans, while Jackson was fearless. At the Battle of Bull Run, the Confederate soldiers had watched Jackson walk into battle calmly, with his head held high and a determined look on his face. His attitude had inspired everyone around him. It seemed as though he had no fear of death.

"Look, men!" another Confederate general had shouted. "There is Jackson standing like a stone wall! Let us determine to die here, and we will conquer."

Thus his nickname, "Stonewall," was born.

Finally, Lincoln found a leader in Ulysses S. Grant. Grant had long been involved in the military and in wars. He seemed to have both the intelligence of Robert E. Lee and the bravery of Stonewall Jackson. Certainly, he had experience in battle and did not fear fighting in a war.

"You want to know what my feelings are on the field of battle?" Grant once explained to a friend. "I do not know that I feel *any* peculiar sensation. War seems much less terrible to persons actually engaged in it than to those who read of the battles."

Whatever Grant's emotions really were when going into battle, he certainly must have felt a great deal of confidence. Soon, his leadership led to wins in critical battles throughout Tennessee. These victories, in turn, allowed him to move further south. His victory at the Battle of Vicksburg in Mississippi is often seen as the beginning of the turning point for the Union. Lincoln was extremely pleased with Grant, but Grant was not without his critics.

"Sir, we've heard again and again that he drinks too much," a Cabinet member, speaking of Grant, said carefully to Lincoln.

Lincoln sighed and looked around the room with a bored expression. "I suppose it *is* unwise to be dehydrated in the midst of a civil war," he said sarcastically.

Another member disregarded Lincoln's comment and added, "I've heard that Grant can drink twelve bottles of whiskey in one evening."

"Well, then," Lincoln said with mock seriousness, "let me know what brand of whiskey Grant uses. If it makes fighting generals like Grant, I'd like to get some for distribution."

The first Cabinet member smiled politely and said, "It's just that things seem to be going well, or at least better, now. We can't afford to have an irresponsible general at the lead."

Now Lincoln's humor was wearing thin. "Do you gentlemen truly not understand that Grant is the reason why this war has taken a victorious turn toward our side? I could not care less if General Grant wants to take a nightly bath in whiskey. I can't spare him—*he* actually fights."

Others criticized Grant for being too cruel in war. He was known for attacking towns and farming areas in the South so brutally that absolutely nothing remained. Once, in instructions to a commander during battles in the beautiful Shenandoah Valley, Grant wrote: *All the farmlands must be destroyed so completely that they can no longer support the Confederate army. Devastate the whole area so thoroughly that a crow flying across the valley will have to carry its own food.*

In his defense, Grant explained that he fought hard and completely in an attempt to end the war, not because he enjoyed the brutal attacks. In fact, like many military officers, he hated war.

"I have never supported war," Grant often said, "except as a means of peace."

Amid all the horror and blood and heartbreak of war, Lincoln was eternally thankful for the playful distraction of his two younger sons, Tad and Willie. Even though the children were now in the White House, Lincoln continued to happily ignore the idea of rules or discipline. The two boys now had a house with thirty-one rooms to tear around in and explore. Immediately, the boys got into as much mischief as they could. They crept into the kitchen as the cook was preparing a state dinner and ate three strawberry pies behind his back. They figured out how the bells and alarms worked in the White House and set off a ringing so severe that Lincoln's secretaries were convinced that a national emergency was taking place. They built a fort on the roof of the White House, to keep an eye out for the rebels, and spent hours making terrific cannon and gun noises.

Tad and Willie were the first children to have ever lived in the White House, and the American public loved them. People could not get enough pictures and stories of Tad and Willie. Many people came to tour the White House (a popular thing to do in 1862) in hopes of getting to see them. The boys had already been spoiled by their own parents, but now they received endless toys, pets, and books from complete strangers.

Even so, both brothers remained sweet and thoughtful—particularly Willie. Of the two boys, Willie was most like his father. He loved to read, care for stray animals, and speak to groups. At only eleven years old, he already knew that he wanted to be a minister when he grew up so that he could help people. Like Lincoln, he often grew quite sad. For these reasons and more, Lincoln had a very tender and special love for his middle son.

It was this love that made the bloody war-filled winter of 1862 a bit more bearable for Lincoln. But then it was also this love that created the darkest hours of Abraham Lincoln's life.

The water around Washington was filthy and full of disease. Thousands and thousands of soldiers were camped around the city, and their waste and garbage eventually seeped into the ground and polluted the water. As a result, many people in Washington came down with typhoid, a very serious disease. In February, both Lincoln boys became very sick with this dreaded illness. Tad recovered slowly, but Willie couldn't seem to shake it. Lincoln would sit for hours by his son's bedside, brushing the damp hair off Willie's forehead and speaking softly to him. On February 20, as Lincoln held his hand, Willie passed away.

"I never saw a man so bowed with grief," a friend of the Lincoln family would later write of Abraham Lincoln. "He lifted the cover from the face of his child, gazed at it long and earnestly, murmuring, 'My poor boy; he was too good for this earth. I know he is better off in heaven—and yet, we loved him so.' Great sobs shook him, and he buried his face in his hands."

Of all the tragedies Lincoln endured during his life, the death of Willie was the hardest. Mary Lincoln was driven nearly to insanity by her own grief. She no longer cared about fancy dresses or silk curtains. Instead, she cut herself off from the rest of the world as she mourned privately inside the White House.

But Lincoln still had a country to attend to. And after Willie's death, something changed in him. He was no longer as patient and careful with the Civil War. He wanted it to end, and he was determined that the North would win so that the United States would remain one country. Also, Lincoln turned his attention once more to the root of the problem in the South: slavery.

For years now, slaves had been risking their lives by running away from their masters to the freedom of the North. Brave leaders like the escaped slave Harriet Tubman had led hundreds and hundreds of slaves along the "Underground Railroad," a path from the deepest South to the line of freedom, the Mason-Dixon Line, in Pennsylvania. But it was a difficult and dangerous path. Many slaves did not survive the journey; others were captured and often beaten or even killed for running away. Lincoln despised the fact that black people were not free to live in the South as the human beings they were. They shouldn't have to *escape* to freedom.

"I want, once and for all, to free the slaves still in bondage in the South," Lincoln announced firmly to his Cabinet one morning in July. "Every day, dozens and dozens of escaped slaves pour into our northern cities. Not only can we not accommodate all of them; they should not have to risk their lives to come here! They should be free in the lands where they now live."

Lincoln then presented his idea for the Emancipation Proclamation. *Emancipation* is another word for *freedom*, so this would be a document proclaiming freedom for all the slaves in the South.

"My plan is to promise that all slaves living in states that are still in rebellion on January 1, 1863, will be freed," Lincoln said, looking each of his Cabinet members in the eye.

His plan met with complete silence. Several men shifted uncomfortably in their seats. For nearly five minutes, no one said a word. Finally, Lincoln's Secretary of State cleared his throat and spoke.

"Mr. President, with all due respect, I think that freeing the slaves right now would appear to be a desperate measure. People will see it as something that will just get overturned if the South wins this war. It won't be taken seriously. We may have turned the tide with Grant's winning some key battles, but we need a huge and decisive victory."

Lincoln's eyes blazed with the same fierceness that, years earlier, the young boys who had been torturing the turtle had seen.

"Then we must win that victory, my friends," Lincoln said in a controlled but emotional voice. "We *must* win."

The Emancipation Proclamation would not change the law. Slavery would still be legal in the Confederate states; only an amendment to the Constitution could change that. But Lincoln, through his power as President, could free the existing slaves. And, after all, he had spent much of his political career speaking out against slavery and promising to do his part to end it. Now the time had come to keep his word.

Eight weeks after presenting the Emancipation Proclamation idea, the North won the huge victory it needed—in the bloodiest one-day battle of the Civil War. At the Battle of Antietam in Virginia, nearly 25,000 soldiers were killed in twelve hours. There were so many deaths that long trenches were dug, and the bodies of the dead were piled in them for mass burials. Parts of the battlefield were ankle-deep in blood.

Lincoln visited Antietam to congratulate the troops, but it was with a sort of grim joy that he celebrated the Union victory. He walked sadly through the fields of dead young men with his tall hat in his hands and tears in his eyes. Like many of his generals, he too hated war. But, even more, he hated slavery and the idea of his country being torn apart. Now, at last, he could do something about the issue of slavery.

Upon returning to Washington, Lincoln wrote the Emancipation Proclamation, decreeing that on New Year's Day, 1863, all slaves in the Southern states would be freed. He also added that black men, then, would be allowed to join the Union forces and fight in the war. Reaction to the Proclamation was immediate: some people were thrilled, while others hated it. It freed slaves only in the South, so some felt it was unfair. Some abolitionists wanted Lincoln to give *more* to the slaves than just their freedom. Others felt black men should not be given the choice to fight in the war.

Lincoln lay sick in bed as news of the reaction came back to him. He had contracted smallpox, a dangerous disease in 1863, during his visit to the Antietam battlefield. Still, as he read about how some people felt that the Proclamation gave either too much or too little, his humor did not fail him. "At least now," he said wryly, referring to his highly contagious disease, "I have something I can give to everyone."

News of the Emancipation Proclamation spread more slowly through the Deep South. Slave owners were in no hurry to let their "property" know about the upcoming day. But bit by bit, the word spread, whispered from cabin to cabin and through the fields. The few slaves who could read, secretly pulled newspapers out of the garbage and learned the news. Around fires at night, young black men appeared from other plantations with the story of Mr. Lincoln and his Proclamation.

To the black men and women who had been slaves all their lives, the news was unbelievable. Freedom would be theirs at last! Was it possible? For three months, slaves from Florida to Virginia counted the days and the hours and the minutes. Some free black leaders in the North thought that Lincoln's promise to sign the Proclamation on New Year's Day was only a political game. They said they'd believe his promise when he kept it.

On New Year's Day, black people gathered in churches throughout the North and South, waiting for the news. In Washington, Lincoln held a large party at the White House that went on for hours. He shook so many hands that day that his own hand was shaking as he walked to his office that night to sign the Proclamation.

"If my hand trembles as I sign my name, people will say I was afraid," Lincoln said to aides and Cabinet members standing around him.

"But you are not afraid, are you, Mr. President?" one young aide asked.

Lincoln smiled. "No. I am not afraid," he said quietly. And with that, he signed the document that freed more than four million black men, women, and children.

Up in Massachusetts, Frederick Douglass had been waiting in Boston's Tremont Temple with hundreds of other black people for nearly twenty-four hours. Douglass was an escaped slave who had taught himself to read and write and, over the years, had become one of the most famous speakers and writers in the United States. He had been known to criticize Lincoln for being slow to take action and for not doing enough to help the slaves. Now, as night fell, Douglass began to wonder if, once again, Lincoln would not take action. All around Douglass, the faces of black people had gone from hopeful to worried to disappointed. Perhaps this Emancipation Proclamation *was* too good to be true, after all.

But, suddenly, a man ran into the church, shouting and ringing a bell.

"The Proclamation is coming! The news is

on the wires! It has happened!"

The hundreds gathered burst into shouts, cheers, weeping, and then song: *Sound the loud timbrel over Egypt's dark sea, Jehovah has triumphed: His people are free!*

As the crowd settled, Douglass stood tall and spoke loudly in his deep, rich voice. "My friends, if Abraham Lincoln has taught us to confide in nothing else, he has taught us to confide in his word."

A month or two later, Lincoln was again hosting an event at the White House. It was a mild winter evening, and the doors of the White House were open so that guests could come and go easily. Slowly, a hush came over the richly attired crowd. They all turned to look at the doorway. Standing timidly just outside the door was a group of black children. Behind them, older black children and a few adults also stood nervously.

Since Lincoln had signed the Proclamation, children often gathered outside the White House, hoping to get just a glimpse of the man who had set them free. Adults were more reluctant to do this, so they usually remained at a distance behind their children. More often than not, Lincoln would walk outside to greet his young admirers.

"What are these dirty little Negroes doing here?" one guest whispered to another. "Someone should call the guards." In spite of their support of the liberation of slaves, many white people still felt that black people should not mix with white people in any way. Certainly, black children should not be allowed anywhere near the White House.

Just then, Lincoln turned to look at the children. A broad smile lit up his face as he moved through the stunned crowd of rich and important people, ignoring their disapproval. Lincoln stooped over as far as he could so that he might be face to face with the children. As he spoke quietly to them, some guests were so disgusted that they walked out.

But Lincoln barely noticed. He was too busy shaking each small hand.

Chapter 12

It was close to midnight in a desolate valley not far from the Smoky Mountains in east Tennessee. A light snow fell on a group of Confederate soldiers as they huddled around a fire, talking in low voices. One young soldier, a boy barely sixteen years old, pulled a package out from under his heavy gray coat and handed it to an older soldier next to him.

"What you got here?" the older man asked, shaking the package.

The boy's eyes twinkled. "It's chocolate. A big block of it, too. Reckon Christmas Eve is as good time as any to break it out. Been hauling it around for darn near twenty days now."

The other soldiers laughed. Chocolate was a rare treat in the middle of a cruel war. It was now December 1864, and the Civil

War had continued to drag on without mercy. Six months earlier, the Battle of Gettysburg, the worst battle of the war, had been fought. Tens of thousands of men had died. And the Confederates had lost. Bit by bit, the Union forces were winning, but even the Union soldiers rarely felt like celebrating. Everyone, both winners and losers, had grown terribly weary of war.

The chocolate was passed around quietly. No one said anything for quite a while; everyone was lost in lonesome thoughts of family and friends miles away. It didn't feel much like Christmas Eve, sitting around on the cold ground in ragged clothing. Many of the men were in bandages and casts. Some of them were sick. All of them were hungry. At least there was chocolate.

Then, from somewhere a bit farther down in the dark valley, came the most unexpected sound: singing. *Silent night, Holy night* . . . It sounded like men's voices. Some of the Confederate soldiers looked at each other, got up, and crept slowly toward the singing. In a clearing, quite close, was a group of Union soldiers, also huddled around a fire. They were singing quietly and also passing food around. The Confederate soldiers listened for a while and then did something that was, in fact, not terribly unusual at this point in the Civil War: they wandered over to their enemy's camp and sat down with them.

For more than an hour, the boys and men sang together and shared food and news. They were fighting on opposite sides in a war, but they were all the same inside. They all missed their homes at Christmas. Before heading back to their separate camps, they shared a prayer for the war to end soon. In the next few days, they would meet on the battlefield, perhaps in a fight to the death against one another. But tonight, they shared one last song: *Sleep in heavenly peace.*

Lincoln knew all too well how much the country longed for peace. No one wanted it more than he did. After the horrible Battle of Gettysburg, in which 40,000 soldiers were killed or wounded, an old man, his eyes filled with tears, came up to Lincoln.

"I've lost my son, Mr. President. He was my only boy."

Lincoln told the old man how terribly sorry he was. Then there was a moment of silence. Lincoln put his hand on the man's shoulder and said, "When I think of the sacrifices of life still to be offered, and the hearts and homes to be made lonely before this terrible war is over, my heart is like lead. I feel at times like hiding in a deep darkness."

Not long after this, the battlefield of Gettysburg was to be memorialized by turning it into a National Soldiers' Cemetery. The battle had been fought in the worst heat of the summer, so all the men killed in battle had to be buried where they had fallen before they began rotting. When the summer rains came, however, some of the bodies were uncovered. The governor of Pennsylvania decided that this was no way to honor fallen soldiers, so he asked that the field become a cemetery.

On a clear, cold November morning, Lincoln spoke to the 9,000 people gathered on the Gettysburg battlefield for the dedication of the cemetery. The field was still scattered with the skeletons of horses and the unfinished coffins of soldiers. Lincoln looked out across the somber crowd, and then he began to speak in his high, clear, emotional voice:

"Fourscore and seven years ago our fathers brought forth on this continent a new nation, conceived in liberty and dedicated to the proposition that all men are created equal . . ."

Barely 286 words long, this may have been one of the shortest speeches Lincoln ever gave, and yet it touched people deeply. His main message was that the soldiers had given their lives so "that the nation might live." The dedication of the field to the soldiers' memory, Lincoln said, was nothing compared to the dedication these young soldiers had shown to their country.

"These dead shall not have died in vain," Lincoln concluded. "Government *of* the people, *by* the people, *for* the people shall not perish from this earth!"

The crowd stood and clapped for a full five minutes. Even so, Lincoln felt that it was not a very good speech.

"I should have spent more time working on it," he humbly confided to a friend later that afternoon. Little did Lincoln know that his Gettysburg Address would become one of the most famous and best-loved speeches ever given in the United States.

The Confederacy was dying. And slowly, Grant's troops moved closer and closer to capturing Richmond, the capital of the Confederacy. If the Union could topple Richmond, the war would be won. It was now just a matter of time.

As the Union forces continued to win battles, Lincoln often went to the army camps to visit the soldiers and the wounded. Sometimes he told them stories and brought news from other camps. Sometimes he simply shook hands and thanked the men. Nearly always, however, Lincoln tried to get a laugh out of the soldiers. Making fun of his own unusual looks never failed to entertain the troops. After all, there was Lincoln in a black suit and ridiculous hat in the middle of an army camp. More often than not, his coat was wrinkled and his pants dusty.

"I have stepped out upon this platform that I may see you and that you may see me, and in the arrangement I have the best of the bargain," Lincoln joked as he stood in front of the soldiers.

However, Lincoln was firm with his generals. He had no patience with either too little confidence or too much bragging. A general who appeared frightened or weak was usually replaced. And a general who was too cocky was often put in his place. One general in particular, Joseph Hooker, followed Lincoln around during a visit, bragging loudly about how he would win every battle coming up. Annoyed, Lincoln finally turned to Hooker.

"General, do you know why the hen is the wisest of all animal creation?" Lincoln asked blandly.

Soldiers had gathered around to hear the answer. Hooker looked confused and shook his head. "No sir."

"Because she never cackles until the egg is laid," Lincoln replied, with a slight wink to the soldiers.

Again, Lincoln managed to get a laugh out of the soldiers—though they had to hide it behind their hands.

There was unfinished business, and Lincoln decided it was best to get started on this business before the next presidential election rolled around.

"It is time to change the Constitution and outlaw slavery forever in the United States," Lincoln said one morning, as he and his Cabinet met at the Capitol. "I believe we can all agree that the Confederacy is not going to win this war and reverse the Emancipation Proclamation. We must move ahead. I would like to have this written into the Constitution after the election."

Lincoln's Cabinet members nodded in agreement with him, though a few seemed uneasy with Lincoln's plan.

"Sir," one Cabinet member began slowly, "do you really think you can win a re-election with the South as angry as it is? Certainly, with the emancipation of the slaves, the South will not be as willing to engage in peace talks once this war is over. If it appears that the South is too unhappy and will not agree to terms of peace, it will keep people from voting for you."

There was dead silence in the room. Lincoln turned slowly to look directly at the Cabinet member who had spoken. "What, exactly, are you saying?"

"It's just . . ." the man spoke hesitantly. "Have you considered reversing the Emancipation Proclamation so that you might win re-election? If the country sees that the South is more willing to agree to peace, it will look better for you. After winning, you could go ahead with the amendment and so on."

Lincoln sat quietly for a moment and then simply said, "No. I would never do that," before calmly moving on. But later he would angrily write: *I should be damned in time and in eternity if I chose soothing the South over keeping my pledge of freedom to the slaves.* Lincoln had never been a man who placed his own political ambitions ahead of what he felt was right, and he was not about to start being that kind of man. Regardless of the upcoming presidential election, Lincoln remained on the same path, moving ever closer toward the goals of unifying the country and ending slavery.

In keeping with this direction, Lincoln drew up what would soon become the thirteenth amendment to the United States Constitution.

On December 6, 1865, the words "Slavery shall not exist in the United States" were written into the Constitution. Now all slaves were free—in both the South and the North. Never again would enslaving another human being be allowed in our country.

"I love the Southern people more than they love me. My desire is to restore the Union. I do not intend to hurt the hair of a single person in the South if it can possibly be avoided."

Lincoln spoke earnestly to crowds in the weeks leading up to the presidential election. He was campaigning not so much for re-election as for his plan to restore peace in the United States. Lincoln was well aware that many politicians were angry with the South and, once the Civil War ended, would love nothing more than to teach Southerners a lesson. Many politicians favored punishment for the Southern states, but Lincoln never felt this way. He knew that there was terrible heartbreak and resentment on both sides. Certainly, creating more pain for the South would not help the country heal.

Many politicians called Lincoln weak because he favored peace, not revenge. But when Election Day rolled around, Lincoln won the presidency again by a wide margin. Regardless of what the politicians might say about Lincoln, the people of the United States loved him. Soldiers, in particular, had turned out by the thousands to vote for their commander-in-chief. Lincoln was affectionately called "Father Abraham" and "Uncle Abe" by the troops; his heartfelt visits to the soldiers, often risking his own health and safety, had meant the world to these young men. They were glad to repay Lincoln's kindness with their votes.

However, others were terribly upset by Lincoln's re-election. Death threats poured in from the South, but this time, Lincoln did not find any of the threats amusing. Some people wrote to say that he would not live through the first year of his second term. Others wrote to say that he would not even live to see his second inauguration. Lincoln asked his bodyguard, Ward Hill Lamon, to keep a close watch.

"How close?" Lamon asked, not long after the election.

"Well, I'd prefer that you not sit in my lap. But try to stay as close as possible for just a bit," Lincoln responded.

For many nights, Lamon slept on the floor right outside of Lincoln's bedroom. Even in sleep, Lamon held a pistol in one hand and a knife in the other.

"With malice toward none, with charity for

all . . . let us strive on . . . to bind up the nation's wounds; to care for him who shall have borne the battle, and for his widow, and his orphan—to do all which may achieve and cherish a just, and a lasting peace."

In his second inaugural address, Lincoln did everything he could to let the South know that there would be no revenge. There would be no bragging or gloating by the North. Lincoln even suggested that the horrible war might have, in fact, been a punishment sent by God to *both* the North and the South for allowing slavery in the United States. After all, slavery had come to our country in the early 1600s; for more than two hundred years, the entire country had allowed it—not just the South.

But many Southerners found Lincoln's peace offerings to be too little, too late. Much of the South had been utterly destroyed, far beyond what was necessary for victory. Cities like Atlanta, Georgia, and Columbia, South Carolina, had been literally burned to the ground by the Union troops. Soldiers had been cruel and abusive to women and children. And many farms and fertile fields had been demolished just to further damage the South's ability to recover from the war. Mary Chesnut, a young Southern woman who kept a daily diary of her experiences in the Civil War, reflected many

Southerners' feelings when she wrote: "We are going to be wiped off the face of the earth!"

Finally the Civil War ended. Only weeks after Lincoln's inauguration, Grant and his troops surrounded Richmond, Virginia, the Confederate capital. The rebel troops fled the city, some of them setting fire to it as they left so that the Union troops could not have the pleasure of destroying it themselves. Richmond had been the proud jewel of the Confederacy. It was particularly bitter to the soldiers and their general, Robert E. Lee, to see it fall.

When all the rebel soldiers were gone and even the Confederate government had fled, Lincoln wanted to walk through the streets of Richmond.

"Thank God that I have lived to see this!" Lincoln said. "It seems to me that I have been dreaming a horrid dream for four years, and now the nightmare is gone. I must go see Richmond."

It must have been a strange experience for Lincoln. As he walked through the smoldering ruins, hundreds of freed slaves surrounded him, smiling and singing. In one morning's brief walk, Lincoln saw both the agony and the ecstasy that the Civil War had brought.

On April 9, 1865, Grant and Lee sat down together in a courthouse in Appomattox,

Virginia. Lee agreed to all the conditions of surrender, but there was no great joy for Ulysses S. Grant. "I feel only sadness at the downfall of a foe who had fought so long and valiantly and had suffered so much for a cause," Grant would later say.

And as Grant walked out into the cold spring afternoon to announce the victory to the Union troops, he raised his hand for quiet. There would be no cheering. He would not allow any victory salutes to be fired from guns and cannons. Not one shot. Grant demanded respect for the defeated Southern armies.

"The war is over. The rebels are our countrymen again," he said somberly. "We are all brothers again."

Four years and 620,000 lives later, the guns of the Civil War were finally silent.

Chapter 13

"I had the strangest dream a few days ago," Lincoln said to Mary on April 13th, only days after the surrender at Appomattox. It was not unusual for Lincoln to tell Mary about his dreams, but something odd in his voice troubled her.

"Strange in what way?" Mary asked, looking at her husband closely. If a war could be read in the lines on a person's face, Lincoln's face would have told quite a long story. The four years had been tremendously hard on the president, and he had aged greatly.

"Well," Lincoln said and then paused. "Perhaps I shouldn't speak of it."

Now Mary was intrigued. "Of course you should speak of it if it bothers you."

Lincoln proceeded, then, to describe an

eerie dream. In the dream, he woke up in his own bed to the sounds of voices and crying downstairs in the White House. But when he wandered downstairs, he could find no people, even though the sounds of mourning continued. Finally, he walked into the East Room. There, a horrible sight met his eyes. Soldiers stood in a circle guarding a casket, while a group of people cried pitifully.

"Who is dead in the White House?" Lincoln had asked a soldier in his dream.

"The president," the soldier replied. "He was killed by an assassin."

As soon as the soldier said this, a loud wail rose from the group of people. Lincoln had awakened at this point.

"The memory of that dream still bothers me, days later," Lincoln concluded.

Mary stared at Lincoln when he finished speaking and then shook her head. "What a horrid dream! I'm glad I don't believe in dreams, or I would be terrified."

"Yes, it was only a dream," Lincoln said. "The sooner we both forget it, the better."

That night, Lincoln and Mary went to bed quite early, both of them exhausted from months of stress and worry that had finally come to an end. The next morning, Lincoln awoke and commented that he had slept more soundly than he could remember in a long time.

"You do seem remarkably cheerful this morning," Mary said with a smile. "No more bad dreams last night?"

"No dreams at all," Lincoln replied. Then he looked out at the beautiful spring morning. Cherry blossoms filled the trees, and sunlight poured down. It was Good Friday and a short day of work for the president and his Cabinet.

"Mary," Lincoln said thoughtfully, "we should go for a carriage ride through the gardens this afternoon and then go to the theater tonight. It's time to have some fun for a change."

"You *are* cheerful," Mary said happily.

"We must *both* be more cheerful in the future," Lincoln said seriously. "Between the war and the loss of our darling Willie, we have both been terribly miserable. That all changes, starting today."

Lincoln's bodyguard, Lamon, was away on vacation. Before leaving, Lamon had warned the President not to attend the theater or any kind of event that would put him in the middle of a crowd.

"Sir, there have been just too many death threats. It isn't safe," Lamon had said.

Lincoln had waved Lamon's warning off. "If I am killed, I can die but once; but to live in constant dread of it is to die over and over."

The fact was, however, that Lincoln was quite concerned that there might be an attempt on his life. The negative reactions to his re-election, the loss of the Civil War by the South, and the addition of the Thirteenth Amendment had truly pushed some people over the edge. Still, Lincoln felt that he must continue to live his life. He would not allow others' hatred to force him into a life of fear and hiding.

That night, the theater was packed for the performance of a popular play called *Our American Cousin.* Many of Washington's politicians and dignitaries were in the audience. The Lincolns sat in the presidential box along with two friends, Clara Harris and her fiancé, Major Henry Rathbone. General Grant and his wife had originally been invited to accompany the Lincolns, but they had had to turn down the invitation at the last minute.

Also in the audience that evening was a young actor named John Wilkes Booth. Booth had been secretly following Lincoln around for nearly four months, studying him and learning his habits and plans. But Booth was no fan of Lincoln's. On the contrary, Booth was violently anti-black and pro-South, and he blamed Lincoln for the fall of the Confederacy. He was particularly upset with Lincoln's recent idea of giving the right to vote to freed slaves. As a result, Booth had been focusing on one dark goal for months: killing President Lincoln.

During that afternoon, Booth had wandered through the empty theater. Because Booth was a fairly well-known actor, no one who worked at the theater questioned him. Why *wouldn't* an actor be in a theater? But Booth's reason for being there had nothing to do with the play that evening.

Booth found the door to the presidential box. Carefully checking to make sure no one was watching, Booth drilled a small hole in the door so that he would be able to observe the President that night. Booth planned a surprise attack on the President. All that would stand in his way would be the guard outside the door, but Booth knew that Lincoln's personal bodyguard was out of town. Perhaps the replacement guard would not be very good.

As bad luck would have it, the guard that evening was one of the worst, both lazy and a drunk. He sat in his chair by the door for only a short time and then decided to take a stroll around the theater in search of whiskey. Immediately, Booth crept to the door and peered in to see where Lincoln was seated. Then Booth quietly opened the door, stepped directly behind Lincoln, and shot him in the back of the head.

Mary and Clara screamed, "They have shot the President!" as Lincoln slumped forward, unconscious. Major Rathbone attempted to tackle Booth, but Booth stabbed Rathbone in the chest and broke free. While most murderers would want to escape without being seen, Booth wanted to make something of a drama out of his escape; he wanted to put on a show no one would ever forget. He leaped from the box down to the stage as hundreds of people in the audience watched in horror.

"*Sic semper tyrannis*!" Booth shouted, waving his pistol and bloody knife. This was Virginia's state motto, meaning "Thus always to tyrants." To Booth, Lincoln had been the tyrant. Then Booth also shouted, "The South is avenged!" and ran off the stage as quickly as he could with a broken leg. He had caught the spur of his boot on a flag during his jump, twisting his leg badly. But before anyone in the stunned audience could react, Booth was on his horse and riding quickly into the night.

"The wound is mortal. It is impossible for him to recover." The doctor tending to

Lincoln shook his head sadly as he spoke to the roomful of family, Cabinet members, and friends. Immediately following the shooting, Lincoln had been carried across the street to the home of a friend. Everyone could see that the gunshot wound was so severe that taking the time and effort to get Lincoln to a hospital would have been pointless. So they laid Lincoln down in one of the upstairs bedrooms, his legs so long that he had to lie diagonally on the bed.

All night, people close to Lincoln gathered at his bedside in tears. He was still barely alive, but unconscious. Mary begged her husband to speak to her, to wake up.

"His dream was prophetic! It *did* come true!" she cried out over and over again. As the night wore on, Mary became so hysterical that the doctor finally moved her to another room and gave her medicine to help her sleep.

Outside the house, a steady rain began to fall, but hundreds of people gathered anyway. They stood in a vigil all night, praying for their fallen president. Soldiers in uniform lined the street, hoping for a miracle for their "Father Abraham." But just after sunrise the next morning, Lincoln struggled to breathe for just a moment, and then he died. The roomful of mourners fell silent as heads bowed. Then

Lincoln's Secretary of War, Edwin Stanton, quietly acknowledged the greatness of the man who had just died by saying, "Now he belongs to the ages."

John Wilkes Booth had not acted alone. The plan had been to murder not only the President, but also Vice President Andrew Johnson, Secretary of State William Seward, and Ulysses S. Grant. The other assassins, however, either lost their nerve or bungled their murder attempts.

After shooting Lincoln, Booth fled on horseback into the countryside. He rode all night, grimacing with the pain of a badly broken leg. Finally, he stopped at a doctor's house to have his leg attended to in the morning. The doctor, Samuel Mudd, claimed to have had no idea at the time that he was treating the man who had assassinated Lincoln. But later it would be discovered that Mudd and Booth had been friends—perhaps Mudd was part of the conspiracy too.

Although Booth had been successful in his assassination attempt, he made a big mistake as he rode into Virginia. All along, Booth had assumed that Southerners, and particularly Confederates in the state of Virginia, would think of him as a hero. Booth thought that as soon as he reached Virginia, he would be safe and surrounded by people who would forever honor him and protect him. He was dead wrong.

Both Union and Confederate soldiers, who worked together voluntarily, tracked Booth down. Ten days after shooting Lincoln, Booth was cornered in a tobacco barn on a Virginia farm. When he refused to surrender, the soldiers set the barn on fire. Even as he lay dying, Booth was convinced that he had done the right thing and was a hero. "Tell my mother I died for my country," Booth whispered, seconds before he died.

Lincoln was to be buried back at his home in Springfield, Illinois. A funeral train carrying his coffin would slowly travel, in reverse, the same tracks Lincoln had traveled four years earlier on his way to the White House. Along the way, Lincoln's open casket would lie in state in a number of cities so that mourners could pay their last respects. This "procession," lasting twelve days, would become known as one of the largest funeral ceremonies in the history of the world:

In Philadelphia, a line of mourners stretched three miles long. It took close to five hours for many to reach Lincoln's coffin.

In New York City, a funeral procession made its way through the center of Manhattan with 75,000 people joining in the march. Storefront window seats that looked out over the procession sold for $100. Entire buildings were draped in black material.

In Chicago, 7,000 people an hour streamed by Lincoln's coffin. People were so desperate to say goodbye to Lincoln that small riots broke out as the viewing time neared an end.

In numerous small towns along the route, tens of thousands of people stood gathered by the train tracks, even in the middle of the night, simply to have the chance to throw a single rose at the slow-moving black train. Many people slept by the tracks for days as they waited for the train.

And in Indianapolis, one of the last stops before Springfield, crowds held up banners expressing their sorrow. Perhaps most touching and most truthful was a large banner held by a group of young black men: "Thou art gone. Friend and foe alike appreciate you now." Black people nationwide were particularly heartbroken over the death of Lincoln. Many had come to see him as a savior, something greater than just a human being. His being murdered on Good Friday only reinforced this sentiment.

By the time Lincoln's coffin reached Springfield, nearly seven million people had honored the life of this remarkable man by personally witnessing his funeral train, his coffin, or his face. In 1865, this was a third of the entire population of the United States.

The times following Lincoln's death were not good times for our country. So many young men killed in the Civil War had left a void. The South was in ruins, and many thousands of people were left homeless and poverty-stricken. Bitter feelings between the North and the South would remain for many, many years. And cruel hatred and discrimination was directed at black people by those who were angered by their freedom.

Yet Lincoln had saved the United States from breaking apart. Although war pained him greatly, he had calmly led the country through a truly terrible war, knowing that preserving the country that our forefathers had founded "four score and seven years ago" was worth the price.

Most importantly, Lincoln had done more to end slavery than, perhaps, anyone else in United States history had ever done. In his tireless fight against the bondage of other human beings, Lincoln made many enemies. One of these enemies would eventually make Lincoln pay for his courage with his life. We can only guess that if Lincoln could speak of his own assassination, he would, without a moment's hesitation, say that giving his life for the freedom of others was worth the price.

As Lincoln's coffin was lowered into the ground on that hot May afternoon in 1865, many mourners present remembered the young lawyer who traveled on horseback and told jokes about himself in court. Others recalled the awkward young man who split logs and was afraid of girls his own age. There were even those present who held a picture in their memories of a thin boy in too-short pants who would walk five miles to borrow a book.

And perhaps, as the sun set on that sad day, some even recalled the way Lincoln had finished a speech so many years earlier. Hoping to give strength and encouragement to those he might not see again, Lincoln had quietly said:

"I leave you, hoping that the lamp of liberty will burn in your bosoms until there shall no longer be a doubt that all men are created free and equal."